Reflective Practice

in the Lifelong Learning Sector

Reflective Practice
in the Lifelong Learning Sector

Jodi Roffey-Barentsen
Richard Malthouse

First published in 2009 by Learning Matters Ltd.

British Library Cataloguing in Publication Data
A CIP record for this book is available from the British Library.

ISBN: 978 1 84445 184 5

Cover design by Topics – The Creative Partnership
Project management by Deer Park Productions, Tavistock
Typeset by PDQ Typesetting Ltd, Newcastle under Lyme
Printed and bound in Great Britain by Bell & Bain Ltd, Glasgow

Learning Matters
33 Southernhay East
Exeter EX1 1NX
Tel: 01392 215560
info@learningmatters.co.uk
www.learningmatters.co.uk

Contents

Acknowledgements

We would like to thank Dr Jean Kelly and her colleagues from the Institute for Learning, for their support while writing this book.

We would also like to thank all our students for their contributions, suggestions and ideas, as they form an integral part of this book.

Finally, a warm thank you to Ian Reece, who kindly wrote the foreword.

Foreword

This very useful work, which I have the honour of prefacing, has qualities that relate (a) the concrete approach of the text, and (b) the authors' thorough understanding of the professional development that is required by teachers working in the further education and skills sector of education. These qualities are, unfortunately, less widespread than you might expect in educational literature of this nature.

First, the concrete approach is based on a mixture of theory and practical examples of the use of the theory in the further education and skills sector of education. Such a mixture, which is used throughout the text, relates very clearly to the changes that have recently taken place in this sector. The importance of reflection has been recognised for some time but, until now, individual teachers have mainly remained free to use it or not as they see fit to improve their teaching and the learning of their students. Now, with the advent of the registration of teachers as members of the Institute for Learning, the need for all teachers within the sector to achieve qualified status, and the continuing professional development (CPD) that is required, formal reflection is mandatory. The concepts of 'reflection' and 'CPD' are the central tenets of the book and both are clearly dealt with through their theoretical perspectives and additionally supported by the practice that is required. The various chapters provide the necessary theoretical underpinning as well as expansions of this through the use of factual situations and teaching practices. Such an approach is concrete and ensures that the twin foci are not only understood but can be applied and evaluated by individual teachers.

Secondly, the authors demonstrate a thorough understanding of professional development. The discussions of why CPD is important, again, lays emphasis not only on the theoretical perspectives and suggestions as to what constitutes CPD, but leaves it to the individuals to discover what is appropriate to them to increase their own knowledge and understanding and their learners' learning. At each point, clearly described examples are provided to assist with professional development. Within the CPD chapters, emphasis is laid upon individual teachers considering their knowledge across their subject matter as well as the importance of the manner in which their learners learn. Educational initiatives should stand, or fall, or be modified because of the quality of their effects upon students. These effects are clearly described within the book.

Throughout the chapters of the book are tasks that the reader is invited to undertake. These tasks provide readers with advance organisers to assist with what is to follow as well as with summaries at the end of a section. All of these tasks are relevant to the content and, in themselves, are assisting with the reflective processes, which must be completed to achieve helpful and successful professional development.

Achieving QTLS: Reflective Practice in the Lifelong Learning Sector is a useful addition to assist teachers (i) with the changes that are currently occurring, and (ii) subsequently with CPD.

Ian Reece

Introduction

This book has been written specifically to assist new teachers in the lifelong learning sector in achieving QTLS and with their continuing professional development (CPD). CPD now plays a significant role in this sector. A major element of CPD is reflective practice. However, you need to know what reflective practice is and how to record your reflections: what is actually involved in the process; how do you plan for the future and how is this linked to your professional development?

The Further Education Teacher's Qualification (England) Regulations 2007 and the Further Education Teachers' Continuing Professional Development and Registration (England) Regulations 2007, came into force on 1 September 2007. A new aspect of these regulations makes it compulsory for all teachers in the lifelong learning sector to register with the Institute for Learning (IfL) and report a minimum number of hours of CPD each year. The CPD will be formally recorded and audited. To reflect this new requirement this book will guide new practitioners towards this end.

We aim to introduce and contextualise reflective practice within CPD. It will introduce and define the subject, place it into context regarding new regulations, identify the reflective practice cycle, describe each part of the cycle in detail with reference to relevant academic texts, introduce the concept of professional reflective practice, identify a need for professional reflective practice, state the various types of CPD and detail how to accurately record professional reflective practice. This is a valuable resource for students on initial teacher training programmes, aiming for QTLS status.

The strength of this book lies in its practical approach to the subject, making it particularly suitable for new practitioners in the lifelong learning sector.

How to use this book

Like all books, you can read this one all the way through or dip into it as necessary. The book does follow a logical progression as it guides you through the concepts of reflection, reflective practice to the new professional reflective practice and offers practical advice to assist you in your own practice. Objectives are stated at the start of each chapter to provide an overview of the chapter and to guide your attention to your own learning in a structured way. You will notice that tasks have been set. The purpose of these is to enable you to think around the subject and to begin to reflect. As you may expect, this book is fully and accurately referenced and offers suggestions for further reading. A great deal of thought has gone into the style of the language used.

We have intentionally kept away from the use of jargon that can be confusing. Likewise, abbreviations are explained at the point of use and a list is included to assist you. You will notice that although this book refers to an academic topic, we have intentionally kept away from an overly academic style. We hope you will enjoy your read.

1
What is reflection?

By the end of this chapter you will be able to:

- distinguish between different approaches to reflection;
- explain the difference between common sense reflection, reflective practice and professional reflective practice;
- consider the use of the models that are discussed for your own practice.

Professional Standards

This chapter relates to the following Professional Standards.

Professional Values:

AS 4 Reflection and evaluation of their own practice and their continuing professional development as teachers.

Professional Knowledge and Understanding:

AK 4.3 Ways to reflect, evaluate and use research to develop own practice, and to share good practice with others.

Professional Practice:

AP 4.2 Reflect on and demonstrate commitment to improvement of own personal and teaching skills through regular evaluation and use of feedback.

AP 4.3 Share good practice with others and engage in continuing professional development through reflection, evaluation and the appropriate use of research.

Introduction

With the introduction of the Institute for Learning, those teaching in the lifelong learning sector now have to partake in and reflect on their professional development. If you are a full-time teacher you are expected to show evidence of at least 30 hours of continuing professional development (CPD) each year. If you work part-time, or as a sessional teacher, the hours are pro-rata equivalent, with a minimum of six hours' CPD. Most of us already engage in CPD as we attend training days or sessions, follow a short course or even embark on a longer programme, such as a degree course or a Masters degree in our specialist subject area. The difference now is that we not only need to attend these events but we also need to reflect on them and record those reflections. As a result, the need for personal reflection on skills, knowledge and attitudes, as well as the identification of personal values, organisational skills, critical thinking and personal change management, has increased. This is achieved through a process called reflective practice, or more precisely, professional reflective practice, a term which is explained later in this chapter.

Theories of reflection and reflective practice

Let's look at reflection and reflective practice in more detail and consider some of the concepts and underpinning theories in relation to the topic. First of all, can it be defined?

TASK TASK **TASK** TASK **TASK** TASK **TASK** TASK **TASK** TASK **TASK** TASK

What do you understand by the term 'reflection'? How would you define it?

Different authors and theorists have offered a range of definitions. These definitions some-times seem similar and some appear to overlap. For the purpose of this book, we will distinguish between three approaches to reflection. Firstly, we discuss 'common sense reflecting', which is familiar to us all as being the way in which we think about and mull over something after, for example delivering a lesson. Secondly, we consider the discipline of thinking about something in a more ordered fashion: we will call this 'reflective practice'. In this part of the chapter we will discuss the works of a number of theorists who have been highly influential in this area. Thirdly, we link reflective practice to CPD. This is called professional reflective practice It is this method or approach to reflection that is required by the Institute for Learning as evidence for the CPD activities that you have undertaken. The concept of professional reflective practice is illustrated by a practical model, the professional reflective practice cycle, which consists of four parts. These four parts, experience, reflection, professional practice and action plan, are described in detail later. Lastly, as you engage in professional reflective practice, you may encounter issues such as problem-solving, personal values, organisational skills, critical thinking and personal change management. They are examples of some of the fundamental skills required by a teacher and will be considered in general terms.

Common sense reflecting

This first approach to reflection is described by Moon (2004, page 82) as the *common sense view* of reflection, which uses the everyday meaning of the verb 'to reflect'. She explains that *reflection is akin to thinking but with more added to this* (page 82). It is the thoughts that occur to us during our day-to-day living, perhaps following a difficult lesson or a particularly challenging student. It is the thoughts we cannot put down after a difficult encounter with an aggressive student or the muses we choose to have when we feel we could do better and try to work out exactly how. After these events, you may think about the situation in terms of what went well and what did not. You could consider the behaviour of the students or how well a particular exercise went. The word 'reflection' is used in this context to represent the type of reflection found within the image of a mirror. If you were to reflect upon something in this way, you may describe what happened, what you did, what others did in response and what you did after that, and then describe how you felt about it.

What this type of reflection lacks is the element of directed learning from the experience; this type of thinking is vague because the process lacks structure. If you wish to benefit from reflecting in any way, then a clear link has to be made from the past to the future. Arguably you improve your chances of doing better in the future by considering what you have done in the past and deciding what should be done differently. In other words, you need to look backwards to see the way forwards. This may sound obvious, but unless you think about what you have done, you may end up doing the same things again and again, never improving. If you wish to improve as a teacher, then what is required is a form of reflection that is more than just thinking about an experience for a while and then doing nothing more about it. To do it takes time and effort and you may not always like what you see. But not to do it would be a greater waste of your time and effort.

Dewey's reflective thinking

In the first half of the twentieth century the philosopher and educationalist John Dewey introduced the concept of reflective thinking. His main interest was problem-solving. He observed that when you begin the process of thinking about something, it normally starts with a problem or a worrying or upsetting situation that cannot be resolved. As a result you are left with a feeling of uncertainty or unease and need to stop and take stock of the situation. At this stage you identify the exact nature of the problem, what it was you were attempting to do, what you actually did and what happened. As summarised by Loughran (1996, page 14):

> *Reflection is clearly purposeful because it aims at a conclusion. The purpose of reflecting is to untangle a problem or to make more sense of a puzzling situation; reflection involves working towards a better understanding of the problem and ways of solving it.*

Reflective thinking is not always an easy or indeed a pleasant process because, as Hillier (2005, page 17) points out, *we are actively challenging the comfortable, taken-for-granted parts of our professional selves*. This is because, reflective thinking forces us to be honest with ourselves. We end up asking questions such as, *What did I do? Could I have done better? What did I not do that I possibly could?* In essence we are leaving ourselves open to criticism by the most challenging of critics, namely ourselves. If we are totally honest, we are forced to admit that we don't have all the answers, don't always get it right and that we have more to learn.

Reflective practice: Schön

The second approach to reflection is referred to as reflective practice and was introduced by Donald Schön in 1983, Schön referred to what he called reflection-in-action and reflection-on-action. Reflection-in-action refers to a person who is forced to start thinking on their feet as they find that what they are doing is not working as well as they had hoped. For example, if you are teaching a lesson that relies upon role-play and you find the class unwilling to co-operate, the lesson will fall apart very quickly. The reasons for this may be many and varied. However, you do not have the luxury of time to go into the whys and wherefores, because you have a lesson to teach and learning outcomes to cover. Instead you may decide to drop the idea of role-plays and adopt another approach. You could decide, for example, to use discussion, or provide verbal examples for the students to consider. What you have just done is reflection-in-action.

On the other hand, having achieved your learning outcomes by opting to do something other than role-plays, you find yourself with a few moments to spare following the lesson. As you reach for a cup of tea, you mull over what happened. You ask yourself why it was that the students were unwilling to perform the role-plays. Was it the make-up of the class, their general attitude to participation in the classroom, the classroom atmosphere or their confidence? On the other hand, was it something you said or did, and how come it has worked well before with other groups? Or was it perhaps because the learners had a week of role-plays in other lessons and were now bored with them? What you have done is an example of Schön's refection-on-action. You are thinking about the experience after the event, not during it.

> **TASK** TASK **TASK** TASK **TASK** **TASK** TASK **TASK** TASK **TASK** **TASK** TASK
>
> Think of an example where you have reflected in-action and also one for when you reflected on-action. Your self-evaluations after teaching may be helpful here.

Kolb's four-stage model

Schön did not offer a model or structure for this form of reflective practice. However, in 1984, another theorist, David Kolb, introduced his four-stage model of learning. Kolb used what can be described as technical language when describing his model, using terms such as, concrete experience (doing it), reflective observation (reflecting on it), abstract conceptualisation (reading up on it) and active experimentation (planning the next stage). In the figure below, the language has been altered to offer a more accessible version of Kolb's four-stage model of learning.

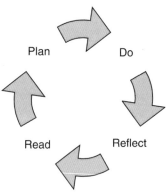

What does this mean for you? How does it work? As can be seen, the model comprises of four stages and it can be applied to any activity. The activity chosen here is teaching a lesson.

Do it	You teach a lesson. Perhaps the lesson is assessed and so you can read the feedback.
Reflect on it	You think about what went well, what went less well, what you did, what you didn't do, the reasons for that, etc. You read the feedback. You identify some topics that require further attention.
Read up on it	You attend your library, search the intranet, internet or speak to your tutor or your peers.
Plan the next stage	Now you have acquainted yourself with the learning theory and suggested good practice you are able to plan how you will design and deliver your next teaching session.

Reece and Walker (2006, page 92) point out that the importance of this model is that it can be started at any stage, it combines reflection with experience and that once started, the cycle should be completed. This model can be very useful for people who are new to teaching. The reason for this is that it is clear, unambiguous and follows a logical progression. For example, if you had not taught a particular session before, it may be appropriate for you to start at the 'read up on it' stage; this would equip you with the knowledge necessary to teach the session. Next you would move to the 'plan next stage'. This would be achieved by identifying your aims and objectives, identifying your methods of assessment, designing a lesson plan, making your personal lesson notes, ensuring you have the resources to hand, identifying the knowledge of the learners considering differentiation and choosing relevant teaching strategies. Next would be to 'do it' and then to 'reflect on it'. But it does not finish there; reflective practice is an ongoing process where you always strive to do a little better on the next occasion. The day you believe it can't get any better is probably the day to stop teaching. So having reflected on it, you now 'read up on it further', and so on and so on.

Kolb offers an effective model for reflective practice. Essentially it means that the teacher, as learner, takes responsibility for his or her own learning. You will notice in the model that there is a time to discuss your views with your tutor or your peers. However, the main thrust of this system is that you take responsibility for yourself. You think about what you have done and how you have done it, and you then read up about it to find more information and decide how you will do it differently on the next occasion. It has been suggested that the only person we really listen to is ourselves; here it is put into practice. This approach to learning is called student-centred learning, because the learner is at the centre of the learning process and assumes responsibility for their learning. Obviously you are not alone while engaging in reflective practice. Your tutor, if you are on a teacher-training programme, will be there to advise, or you may have a mentor, if you are new to teaching. However, ultimately you decide how well you have done and what is required of you on the next occasion in order to make your teaching as effective as it can be.

> **TASK** TASK **TASK** TASK **TASK** **TASK** TASK **TASK** TASK **TASK** **TASK** TASK
>
> Think of an occasion where you have changed or modified your teaching. Looking back, try to identify each of the steps of Kolb's cycle as you went through this process.

Gibbs' reflective cycle

Kolb's model was further developed by Graham Gibbs, who, in 1988, offered another model.

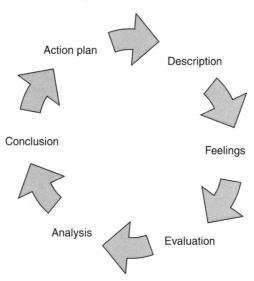

Gibbs' reflective cycle is fairly self-explanatory but in being more descriptive has the effect of restricting the user to consider only the points offered. You will notice that it encourages reflective practice by asking questions at six stages, described below.

1	**Description**	A description of the situation or event.
2	**Feelings**	The feelings of the participant are considered.
3	**Evaluation**	It evaluates the experience by considering what was good and bad about the experience.
4	**Analysis**	Analysis is employed to make sense of the experience and to state what was learned about the event.
5	**Conclusion**	Considers what you could have done differently or in addition.
6	**Action plan**	If it were to happen again, what would you do?

There are a number of other definitions of reflective practice. Boyd and Fales (1983) define reflection as the process of internally examining and exploring an issue of concern, triggered by an experience, which results in a change in perspective. Another definition, offered by Osterman and Kottkamp (1993, page 19), is that *reflective practice is viewed as a means by which practitioners can develop a greater level of self-awareness about the nature and impact of their performance, an awareness that creates opportunities for professional growth and development*. Reflective practice is therefore all about thinking about an experience with a view to gaining an improved understanding of that experience, and involves an ordered, systematic and documented approach with a view to gaining self-improvement. The principal reason for using reflective practice is to improve performance. Osterman and Kottkamp (1993) believe that it is by reflection and analysis that we try to understand an experience.

Brookfield's critical lenses

Stephen Brookfield (1995) identified the importance of researching critically what we do as teachers. He argued that *critically reflective teaching happens when we identify and scrutinize the assumptions that undergird how we work* (page xii). As a teacher, you need to discover and examine your assumptions by looking at your practice, at what you do, through four points of view, or, as described by Brookfield, four 'critical lenses', which are:

1. the point of view of the teacher;
2. the point of view of our learners;
3. the point of view of our colleagues;
4. the point of view of theories and literature.

What Brookfield is doing here is adding a critical element to reflective practice. First you observe from your own perspective, but it does not stop there. Next you include your students by asking them how they perceive your actions and what it is about those actions that they like or dislike. Following this, you ask your colleagues to be *mirrors, mentors or critical friends*. By doing this you are able to enter into more critical conversations about your practice. Often this will highlight areas that until this point had not been considered. Lastly, your practice will take into account reference to theories and literature. Here you compare your own ideas and actions with existing theoretical frameworks.

- Think about the ways in which you can obtain the views of your students.
- Identify a colleague with whom you can have an open and critical conversation about your teaching.
- Your next step is to have the conversation and reflect upon it.

Reflective practice in this sense considers an experience from many angles and perspectives, drawing upon relevant theory to identify an appropriate way forward. What differentiates common sense reflecting from reflective practice is highlighted in the table below.

Common sense reflecting	Reflective practice
No consideration of organisation	The use of the reflective practice cycle
Descriptive writing	Analytical writing
Few or no links to previous reflections	Links to previous considerations
Usually not recorded	May be recorded formally
A solitary process. Not intended to be read by others	Generally a solitary process but ideas may be shared with others
Not used as a developmental tool	It is developmental; mainly personal development
It considers the past more than the future	It is often aspirational in nature
It is self-absorbed	It makes clear links to professional practice
No considerations given for future practice	It employs the use of an action plan

The general differences in the two methods of reflection are that, unlike common sense reflecting, reflective practice produces a learner who is autonomous and improves a person's understanding of the subject, and their critical thinking, problem-solving and individual change management skills. Biggs (1999, page 6) alluded to the mirror analogy, suggesting that *a reflection in a mirror is an exact replica of what is in front of it*. He saw a distinction between this and reflective practice by observing that *Reflection in professional practice, however, gives back not what it is, but what it might be, an improvement on the original*.

Reflective practice is used for the purpose of self-improvement. For example it can be used to consider your performance, academically, socially and psychologically: academically, because there will be occasions when having considered a topic, you realise that you don't know enough about it to make an informed decision; socially, because after reflecting you may identify that your social skills need to be improved in specific areas; and psychologically, because you could find that the way in which you react to situations may need to be adapted.

Professional reflective practice and continuing professional development

Whereas reflective practice is concerned with personal achievement, when combined with CPD it becomes a means by which teachers can extend their knowledge and skills to maintain and increase competence throughout their professional lives. In this context, reflective practice can be extended to professional reflective practice. This term is used to differentiate between the personal reflective practice associated with an individual's development as a teacher and the broader concept within the professional arena. Reflective practice is restricted to your personal development within the classroom. Professional reflective practice, however, extends this concept as it captures the various aspects that influence your role as a teacher upon which you can reflect. There is another important issue here that has to be considered. Whereas reflective practice is concerned with an individual's progress within naturally occurring events, professional reflective practice is reliant upon the individual actively searching for and participating in activities that will improve their professional practice. Tummons (2007, page 69) refers to this as involving *A constant critical appraisal of teaching and learning, and of the work of a tutor more generally*. Professional reflective practice is not restricted to thinking about your learning or teaching alone; it encompasses all aspects of your professional practice. These activities can include meetings, conversations, seminars, internal and external training events, conventions, etc. In essence it can be anything associated with your work. Unlike reflective practice, professional reflective practice must indicate how you have benefited from your experience professionally – it is not sufficient to merely describe a conversation for example. This will be considered in a later chapter. What differentiates professional reflective practice from common sense reflecting and reflective practice is highlighted in the table below.

Common sense reflecting	Reflective practice	Professional reflective practice
No consideration of organisation	The use of the reflective practice cycle (Kolb)	The use of the professional reflective practice cycle
Descriptive writing	Analytical writing	Writing at an analytical, evaluative and synthesised level
Few or no links to previous reflections	Links to previous considerations	Links to previous considerations
Usually not recorded	May be recorded formally	It is recorded formally
A solitary process. Not intended to be read by others	Generally a solitary process but ideas may be shared with others	A shared process therefore it will be read by colleagues and the Institute for Learning
Not used as a developmental tool	It is developmental mainly personal development	It is developmental mainly professional development
It considers the past more than the future	It is often aspirational in nature	It is goal orientated with SMART objectives
It is self-absorbed	It makes clear links to professional practice	It makes clear links to professional practice in a broad sense
No considerations given for future practice	It employs the use of an action plan	It employs the use of an action plan

You will notice that professional reflective practice is not a solitary process; on the contrary, it is best done on a collaborative basis with your peers or colleagues.

Professional reflective practice cycle

To support you with reflecting on your CPD we have designed the professional reflective practice cycle. This forms a pictorial representation to help you understand the process. It shares best practice from Kolb, Schön and Gibbs and introduces elements that are pertinent to your own working environment as you prepare for your QTLS award. It consists of four stages, as shown in the following figure.

This model considers professional reflective practice by drawing on four distinct areas:

1. **Experience**. What actually occurred?
2. **Reflection**. Thinking about the experience.
3. **Professional practice**. How does this relate to my professional practice?
4. **Action plan**. The identification of SMART objectives and an action plan.

Experience

The professional reflective practice cycle usually begins with an experience. This experience can take many forms and does not restrict itself to the classroom environment or to the subject of actual teaching. Here, the considerations open to you form a part of the larger picture and can include your experiences when you are, for example, attending a course, a meeting or seminar. Perhaps you received feedback from your assessor, tutor, mentor or colleague, after delivering a lesson.

Reflection

Following the experience, the next step is to think about it. It is helpful to ask yourself a number of questions such as *What happened? Why did it happen? How did it happen?* Here it is useful to think about the subject from a number of different perspectives. This process can take a number of days as you mull over all the possible causes and effects.

Professional practice

It is useful to have some method of evaluating the experience, for example, you can ask yourself, *How does this relate to my professional practice?* In this instance, evaluating the experience serves to focus your thoughts and provides a natural boundary. The questions that could be asked here include: *What did I learn? How does it relate to my professional practice exactly? What will I do differently as a result of this? What did I like, or not like, and why? How does this relate to me? Am I being objective or subjective? Am I being positive or negative? Why is this?*

Action plan

The final part of the cycle involves the action plan; this can take the form of specific goals. These goals are derived from considerations of your professional practice. Make your goals SMART. In other words, they should be specific, measurable, achievable, relevant and be time-bound. When you have achieved your goals you are then ready for the next experience, and so on.

A SUMMARY OF **KEY POINTS**

In this chapter we have looked at the following by key points.

> **The Institute for Learning requires you to show evidence of continuing professional development.**

> **There are three different approaches to reflection: common-sense reflecting, which is the thoughts that occur during your day to day living, that you mull over and think about. Reflective practice, which asks you to analyse what has happened, think about it, read up about it and plan for the next experience. Professional reflective practice links reflective practice to the professional arena. It requires you to consider an experience, think about it, relate it to your professional practice and finally identify an action plan with SMART objectives ready for your next experience.**

> **We have highlighted the works of Dewey, Schön, Kolb, Gibbs and Brookfield, using these as a base for the professional reflective practice model.**

REFERENCES AND FURTHER READING REFERENCES AND FURTHER READING

If you wish to explore particular theories or perspectives in greater depth, the following are suggested.

Biggs, J (1999) *Teaching for quality learning at university.* Buckingham: Open University Press.

Bolton, G (2005) *Reflective practice: writing and professional development.* London: Sage.

Boyd, E and Fales, A (1983) Reflecting learning: key to learning from experience. *Journal of Humanistic Psychology*, 23 (2): 99–117.

Brookfield, SD (1995) *Becoming a critically reflective teacher.* San Francisco, CA: Jossey-Bass.

Dewey, J (1933) *How we think.* Lexington, MA: Heath.

Gibbs, G (1988) *Learning by doing: a guide to teaching and learning methods.* Oxford: Further Education Unit.

Hillier, Y (2005) *Reflective teaching in further and adult education* (2nd edition). London: Continuum.

Loughran, J (1996) *Developing reflective practice*: *learning about teaching and learning through modelling.* London: Falmer Press.

Moon, J (2004) *A handbook of reflective and experiential learning theory and practice.* London and New York: RoutledgeFalmer.

Osterman, KF and Kottkamp, RB (1993) *Reflective practice for educators, improving schooling through professional development.* Newbury Park, CA: Corwin Press.

Reece, I and Walker, S (2006) *Teaching, training and learning, a practical guide* (6th edition). Sunderland: Business Education Publishers.

Schön, D (1987) *Educating the reflective practitioner.* San Francisco: Jossey-Bass.

Tummons, J (2007) *Becoming a professional tutor in the lifelong learning sector.* Exeter: Learning Matters.

Websites

For information on the LLUK standards and CPD requirements visit:
www.lifelonglearninguk.org
www.ifl.ac.uk

For useful summaries and essays on reflective practice visit:
www.infed.org

2
Why reflect?

By the end of this chapter you will be able to:

- **identify reasons for reflective practice;**
- **explain the meaning of professionalism;**
- **recognise the link between learning and reflective practice;**
- **list the ten benefits of reflective practice.**

Professional Standards

This chapter relates to the following Professional Standards.

Professional Values:

AS 4 Reflection and evaluation of their own practice and their continuing professional development as teachers.

Professional Knowledge and Understanding:

AK 4.3 Ways to reflect, evaluate and use research to develop own practice, and to share good practice with others.

Professional Practice:

AP 4.2 Reflect on and demonstrate commitment to improvement of own personal and teaching skills through regular evaluation and use of feedback.

AP 4.3 Share good practice with others and engage in continuing professional development through reflection, evaluation and the appropriate use of research.

Introduction

As stated by Tummons (2007, page 68): *There's a lot of reflective practice about*. Some people are 'natural reflectors'; they automatically reflect on their actions and practice. Others, though, perceive it as extra work on top of a busy and demanding job. If you hold this view, you may ask: why bother, what are the benefits? This chapter will discuss the reasons and explain some of the benefits of reflective practice.

The first reason is probably extrinsic: you do it because according to the regulations for teachers in the lifelong learning sector you have to. On the other hand, the reasons can be intrinsic: you want to improve your teaching practice, become more professional or be empowered. In addition, you will recognise that reflective practice benefits your own learning, problem-solving skills, your critical thinking, decision-making, organisational skills or your personal change management. Whatever the origins of your motivation, it is likely that as a consequence of engaging in reflective practice you will increase your knowledge and understanding of yourself as well as your teaching.

Reasons for reflective practice

As previously mentioned, the first reason is probably an extrinsic one: the regulations require you to engage in reflective practice. As discussed in Chapter 1, the Institute for Learning (IfL) requires all full-time teachers, trainers and tutors in the lifelong learning sector to complete and record at least 30 hours of CPD per year (pro-rata for sessional/part-time teachers). To explain the philosophy behind CPD it is useful to consider the following: would you visit a doctor (GP), who, after qualifying years earlier, has taken no interest in new developments in the profession? The answer is probably no. You want a GP who is aware of the latest medicines, treatments and therapies now available for your benefit. The same argument is used with teachers. It isn't enough to get qualified; you also next need to engage in CPD. However, the CPD activities you choose to undertake will only count towards your 30 hours if you can critically reflect on what you have learned; how you have applied this to your practice; and how it has impacted on your learners' experience and success (IfL, 2007a, page 10). Commitment to CPD and critical reflection therefore contribute to maintaining your 'professional standing'. In other words, reflective practice is part of being professional.

TASK TASK **TASK** TASK **TASK** **TASK** TASK **TASK** TASK **TASK** **TASK** TASK

Think about professionalism and answer the following questions.

- What is professionalism?
- What does it mean to you?
- What things go together to make a professional?
- What separates a professional from non-professionals?

Professionalism

There are a number of definitions of professionalism. The most minimal definition describes being a professional as being paid for doing a job (Armitage et al., 2003, page 5). Further to that, it also implies subject knowledge and a degree of responsibility. Freidson (2001, page 17) states succinctly: *professionalism is a set of institutions which permit the members of an occupation to make a living while controlling their own work.* The notion of controlling your own work is also referred to as self-regulation. Similar in some aspects, Joycelyn Robson (2006) offers three component parts of professionalism, namely:

- professional knowledge;
- autonomy;
- responsibility.

She asserts that professional knowledge relates first to the teacher's subject knowledge and second to knowledge of teaching, learning, psychology and sociology. You must be qualified and experienced in your own subject area but you must also demonstrate expertise and skill in the field of education and teaching. Teachers in the lifelong learning sector are often professionals in their own field before they start their teaching career. For instance, you could be an engineer; working in childcare; or maybe the travel and tourism industry, before considering teaching your subject. In this sector therefore, there are two parts to your professionalism. This is referred to as 'dual professionalism'. First there is your subject specialism (engineering, childcare, travel and tourism, etc). Second there is the 'teaching and learning' component of your professionalism. Both parts of your professional practice are equally important. You therefore need to keep abreast of changes and developments in your own subject specialism, as well as in teaching and learning, by taking an active interest in your own professional development.

The second component is that of autonomy. As a teacher you will have to be in a position to deal with the many and varied situations that occur within the classroom environment. When these situations arise, inevitably there is no one to turn to but you. It is your experience and judgement that will enable you to deal with the situation. However, with that autonomy comes the third component: responsibility. You have a responsibility to ensure that you behave in an appropriate way; you don't use the classroom as, for example, a platform to espouse your political or religious beliefs. You have a responsibility to take appropriate action when others misbehave in your class, to challenge inappropriate behaviour whether done intentionally or as a joke, and to ensure fairness and impartiality. To ensure a unified expectation of behaviour and conduct across the sector, the IfL developed a Code of Professional Practice which all its members need to adhere to.

To summarise, professionalism results as a consequence of setting high standards, by maintaining appropriate specialist knowledge, and by shared values. To illustrate this, the adoption of high standards has been made possible with the introduction of the Further Education Teachers' Qualifications Regulations 2007; maintaining appropriate specialist knowledge is achieved by commitment to CPD; and shared values are achieved by adhering to the Code of Professional Practice and the associated disciplinary processes. The ultimate aim is for self-regulation (*controlling own work, autonomy*).

The IfL suggest that:

> *If we can create a uniform understanding of professionalism, where all teachers believe that through striving to maintain their good standing they provide the best possible teaching and learning, we can deliver self regulation at the level of the individual practitioner.*

> (IfL, 2007b, page 3)

So far this chapter has concentrated on the extrinsic reasons for reflective practice, as part of your professional standing. There are, however, further advantages to reflecting that may at first not be apparent. These are the intrinsic reasons or motivators; they come from within yourself. The boundaries between extrinsic and intrinsic motivators are not always clear. It may be that you reflect on your CPD activities because you have to (extrinsic), but that being a professional is something you strive towards from within, as it makes you feel better about yourself (intrinsic). These intrinsic benefits may be quite subtle at first and difficult to identify before you embark on reflective practice. You only see the benefits afterwards (after more reflection). They are different for all of us, depending on your personality, background and situation. There isn't a finite list of benefits, or any guarantees. However, you will find that as you begin thinking about issues that are relevant to you, you will employ coping strategies to deal with these issues. And, as a result, you will improve your own capability in areas that before you may not have given much time to.

The next part of the chapter will give you some ideas on the benefits of reflective practice.

> **TASK** TASK **TASK** TASK **TASK** **TASK** TASK **TASK** TASK **TASK** **TASK** TASK
>
> List what you believe to be benefits of reflective practice.

Ten benefits of reflective practice

1. Improving your teaching practice

Reflective practice is an important aspect of your training to become a teacher. This often takes the form of a journal where you are encouraged to reflect upon the various aspects of your teaching. This is done to enable you to start to think about what you are doing. The reasoning behind this is that if you do not think about what you have done, then the chances are you may do the same things over and over without improving. If what you are doing is not effective, then repeating it is not only foolish but arguably a waste of time for all involved in your lesson. On the other hand, if something has gone well in your lesson, it's worth analysing why it went well, what was it that made it work, whether you can do it again, and if it can be further improved. For example, you always teach a subject giving a PowerPoint presentation, used by your colleagues in your department. On one occasion you decided to use a different teaching method, incorporating more 'pair work'. Your learners were all motivated and engaged, there was even a buzz in the class. It may be useful to reflect on why this was: would it work with other groups and subjects? Can it be improved, would groups of three learners be better than pairs? And so on. After each lesson you teach, it is considered good practice to reflect on how that lesson went, in the form of a self-evaluation. You reflect on what went well in that session and why, what could be improved and how you can make that improvement. Areas to focus on include your planning and delivery of the session in terms of learning outcomes – were they appropriate for that lesson, did you meet them?; teaching methods; assessment methods; differentiation; resources; general class-room management; timing; etc. Occasionally you will encounter what is sometimes referred to as a 'critical incident'. This can be either a sudden change for you, something that happened in your class or did not go as expected, or it could be a sudden awareness of perhaps a gradual change. In the example above, the critical incident could be that your PowerPoint wasn't working, or perhaps your usual classroom was used for exams that day and you were allocated a different room without the facilities. Or maybe you felt, over time, that the PowerPoint presentation wasn't always keeping the learners interested, and you therefore decided to try a more student-centred approach. As a trainee or new teacher it can be quite daunting to 'let go' of some of the control. However, on this occasion you felt you were ready to take that step: why was that? In Chapter 3, critical incidents will be discussed in greater detail. However, as is clear from the above, if you are passionate about your teaching, as most teachers are, then reflective practice represents one of the most effective methods of learning available to you.

2. Learning from reflective practice

Is there a link between learning and reflecting? Or more strongly: do you learn by reflecting? The answer is yes, but not necessarily the same on every occasion. You have to consider your own attitude and approach to learning at the time. Moon (2004, page 84) identifies the link between reflection and its role in learning. She refers to a continuum, with a 'surface' approach to learning on one end of the continuum and a 'deep' approach on the other.

Surface learning describes a person who is concerned only with the superficial aspects of a subject, memorising facts. Reflection therefore is limited.

A deep approach to learning involves the learner submersing themselves with the subject matter, seeking to understand its meaning in relation to previous knowledge. Here the subject matter is analysed, links are made, causation, effect and consequence are identified and knowledge is evaluated and transferred. This can only be achieved by commitment to reflective practice. Moon (2004, page 85) further explains the link between reflective practice and learning by referring to the structure of observed learning outcome (SOLO) taxonomy, which was developed by Biggs and Collis in 1982. Within the field of education a 'taxonomy' refers to a hierarchical list. Within this taxonomy there are five levels of understanding; each level increases in complexity. Each level incorporates the level that preceded it and adds a little more to it. The explanations below are described from the perspective of a person engaging in learning; specifically that of knowledge of a car; Moon's titles are placed within quotation marks.

'Noticing' Pre-structural	The person has pieces of knowledge. They do not necessarily understand what they know and they are unable to organise the information. This is like knowing the names of some parts of a car.
'Making sense' Uni-structural	Some connections between the pieces of knowledge are identified but these are tenuous and lack comprehension or awareness. Now it is realised that the steering wheel controls the wheels in some way. Exactly how many wheels and how this is achieved is not known.
'Making meaning' Multi-structural	Now more connections are being made but not enough to make a claim to full comprehension. The relationship between the steering wheel, steering column, axle and wheels have been identified; however, there is no knowledge of differential or the rack and pinion. If this person were given the parts of a car to put together it is unlikely that anything other than modern art would be produced.
'Working with meaning' Relational	All of the connections are made in relation to the whole. The person has a clear idea of the name and function of each component part of the car and can identify the existing relationships between each part of the car.
'Transformative learning' Extended abstract	The person is able to make connections with the specific subject matter and has the ability to go beyond it. As a result they can take a broad view and transfer the principles and ideas to other subject knowledge areas. The person can relate their knowledge of a specific car to that of other cars, mini buses, vans etc.

For more on this subject see Atherton, JS (2005) *Learning and teaching: SOLO taxonomy*. Available at www.learningandteaching.info/learning/solo.htm

The table above lists five approaches to learning, moving from what is referred to as surface learning at the 'noticing' level, to deep learning at the 'transformative learning' level.

The SOLO taxonomy can be used to demonstrate the relationship between reflective practice and learning (Moon, 2004, page 85). The model below identifies the five stages of the SOLO taxonomy. The shaded area indicates the level of reflection associated with each level. The relationship between deep learning (transformative learning) and reflective practice is clear: the deeper the learning, the greater the need for reflective practice. Or thinking about it the other way around, the use of reflective practice will enable you to move through the taxonomy. This is because the use of reflective practice will enable you to understand the subject.

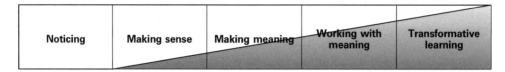

| Noticing | Making sense | Making meaning | Working with meaning | Transformative learning |

You will notice from the model above that reflective practice plays an increasingly important part in the learning process; in fact it is crucial. Without it you would be unable to think around a subject to make those critical connections, you would be condemned to the first stage of the SOLO taxonomy, simply 'noticing'.

3. Enhancing problem-solving skills

It is likely that much of your time reflecting will be spent considering how to solve problems. However, before you can solve a problem, you'll have to recognise there is one, and further to that, identify exactly what the problem is. Problems are often regarded as an indicator of incompetence or even failure; as a result of this, many of us have built effective defences for preventing problem recognition (Osterman and Kottkamp,1993, page 23). In other words, on many occasions, we do not even identify problems because that would mean we would have to face up to our shortcomings. For many, this is not a desirable place to be. However, that is what in part reflective practice is all about, acknowledging the problems that exist and asking yourself whether it is as a result of your own shortcomings or, alternatively, as a result of something externally and not within your control.

If we acknowledge that we may face problems, sometimes of our own doing, we must be equipped to deal effectively with those problems. There are many ways in which we can go about problem-solving, depending on the type of problem and the people involved. Steps in problem-solving follow a general pattern:

1. clarifying and describing the problem *(clarification)*;
2. analysing the possible causes *(analysis)*;
3. considering alternatives *(deliberation)*;
4. choosing one *(selection)*;
5. putting it into practice *(initiation)*;
6. evaluating whether the problem was solved or not *(evaluation)*.

4. Becoming a critical thinker

Critical thinking is best understood as the ability of thinkers to take charge of their own thinking (Elder and Paul, 1994). Being able to think well matters, but it is not something that all of us can do without practice and effort. There is a direct correlation between reflection and thinking critically. In fact many attributes are shared by both. Some typical attributes of a critical thinker are: to ask pertinent questions, to look for proof, to assess statements and arguments, and a sense of curiosity. These qualities, if practised, will inform your practice as a teacher. It is not necessary to have all the answers because the critical thinker is able to acknowledge a lack of understanding but is willing to listen carefully to others. Reflection necessitates an open mind, and in support of this, the critical thinker suspends their judgement until all facts have been gathered and considered, and looks for evidence to support assumptions and beliefs. Reflection will result in a person changing their mind; as a critical thinker they will be able to adjust opinions when new facts are discovered. Lastly, the other attributes of a critical thinker that complement reflection are the ability to examine problems closely and the ability to reject information that is incorrect or irrelevant.

As with problem-solving, your critical thinking skills can be enhanced by the use of reflection. It is the fact that you are actually taking time to think about things rather than rushing off and just 'doing' all the time. Barnett (in Moon, 2004) suggests that reflection actually slows the pace of learning and provides us with what he refers to as intellectual space. Reflection requires the luxury of time for thinking, which can be a new concept for some, but putting time aside to think is important. When we begin to think analytically, our thinking is said to be critical thinking. Critical thinking is a form of discrimination, a way of thinking that is purposeful, producing a considered opinion based on reflection. It gathers information in such a way that you can begin to understand the exact nature of the problem which will in turn provide you with the ability to solve problems, make decisions, and as a result identify options.

5. Making decisions

Decision-making goes hand in hand with problem-solving and critical thinking. There will undoubtedly be times when you have to make a decision as you reflect on your situation. Decision-making is something that can be practised and there are a number of techniques that can assist with this process. These decision-making techniques will help you to make the best decisions possible with the information you have available. They will identify the importance of various factors and the likely consequences of choosing them.

Decision-making is the process of identifying the existence of a problem and finding the most appropriate solution to it. Often though, there will be more than one option to choose from and they may all appear as suitable or unsuitable as each other. Having a set of options is not always a good thing for some people. For example, how are you expected to decide which option is the best for you at any given time in any given circumstance? This is where the application of a process is of use, and we offer a seven-step model.

1. Think about the situation.
2. Identify the problem.
3. Assemble all appropriate information.
4. Develop as many options as possible.
5. Evaluate each to decide which is desired.
6. Decide on the most appropriate option.
7. Put it into action.

6. Improving your organisational skills

It's often said that organisational skills are about having a place for everything and everything in its place, but it is quite possible to have everything in its place and still not be organised. The trouble with study is the huge pressure you may find yourself under due to the vast amount of things that can creep into your life – especially perhaps as you work towards your QTLS and find there is much to read, do, think about, learn, reflect upon, write about (and that's before you even consider your personal life and sleep). Organisational skills are all about not doing certain things so as to make room for the things that are more important. It's about prioritising what there is to do. Inevitably, some things will not get done immediately. If we try to deal with everything that comes our way, we are doomed: we will undoubtedly fail. It is about respecting the reality of a situation. This means perhaps saying no to people and things that you may once have chosen to squeeze in to your already busy life. Organisational skills go hand in hand with time management and time is the most valuable resource you have; once it's gone it's gone.

At work you may find yourself inundated by paperwork. Try this: every time you pick up a piece of paper, put a small tear in it (don't do this with a very important document). After a week look at your paperwork and count the small tears in every piece. You may be surprised by the amount of tears in a paper. Rather than shuffling the paper from one side of you desk to the other, consider dealing with it on the first occasion.

Our organisational skills are useful when we have large or time-consuming projects to complete, for example assignments or portfolios. It is very easy to be put off just by looking at them in their entirety. However, by breaking these projects down into smaller, more manageable pieces (i.e. organising them) they will become easier to achieve. In a way your brain follows a similar routine: rather than making you aware of all the sounds that surround you, it filters them out. As a result, you are made aware of only the important issues for your immediate attention, e.g. someone calling your name, an element of perceived danger, etc. You can do the same by filtering out the tasks that are, at that time less, important than others.

Preparing to be organised includes the need to practise self-management skills and the organisation of your time. This can be achieved by an increased self-awareness of your personal issues in relation to your organisational skills, setting your own standards and taking responsibility for your own actions and behaviour. Remember, you are not alone, you can get information or help from your colleagues and from the various support systems available to you at your place of work.

7. Managing personal change

There is a tendency to become negative about yourself when reflecting. Indeed according to Bolton (2001, page 2), *Reflective practice can fall into the trap of becoming only confession*. This is because you may search for situations that are not going well, so that you can think about them, read up, or research them, then decide how you are going to deal differently the next time the situation occurs. An unintended result of this is that it could make you feel either defensive or disheartened. Schön (1993) turns this on its head, suggesting that:

> When a practitioner becomes a researcher into his [or her] practice, he [or she] engages in a continuing process of self... education the recognition of error, with its resulting uncertainty, can become a source of discovery rather than an occasion for self defence.

> (Schön, in Osterman and Kottkamp,1993, page 54)

Generally people don't like change and when it is forced upon them, they will react to it in differing ways and to differing extents, generally negatively. As a learner, when reflecting you will encounter change, either as a result of a change in your own attitude, as a result of changes forced upon you by your institution or by other factors. Change means loss; in other words, if you have a change in your lifestyle, or find yourself in a new situation, you will have lost an element that made up a part of what you were. This generally brings about a reaction. For some it is hardly noticeable and the change is relatively quick, for others it is a longer and more painful experience. This is what is known as the change process, which is a reaction most of us go through when we experience a loss or change. The extent of the change process depends very much on the nature of the individual and the extent of the change.

Being aware of the process enables us to deal with it when we find ourselves in a place that we don't quite understand. The change process consists of five general steps:

1. shock;
2. denial;
3. anger;
4. rejection;
5. acceptance.

The initial feelings are that of shock. This is displayed in various degrees according to the situation and the person receiving the news. Next may be denial; we say 'may' because not every person exhibits all of these conditions. With the onset of denial, people will prefer not to acknowledge what is obvious to the casual onlooker. They will ignore the situation as if nothing has actually happened in the hope that the new and undesired situation will go away. However, eventually they will have to face reality and when they do the next stage is entered. This next stage is that of anger, which is often associated with feelings of injustice or unfairness. However, by now the fact that change is occurring has actually been acknowledged and is arguably a good thing. It is good because rather than bottling up the emotions, the person can let off a bit of steam. Rejection is experienced when the loss is fully realised and the person can hit a low. Generally over time, the situation is accepted and lastly healing can take place, where what is a state of normality for that individual returns. In general, people have a norm of behaviour with variations, for a person to feel sad or depressed for any length of time can be uncomfortable and so the individual resumes their normal pattern of behaviour. Interestingly, a person can and often does return to previous steps in the process, most noticeably back to anger as they think back to the issue and relive the feelings.

This may sound a little dramatic, but it happens frequently to people to a greater of lesser degree – many are just unaware of what is happening. If you have felt an injustice when things have changed and over which you had no control, you could have been experiencing this process. The root cause of this can involve many aspects of your life including your learners, peers, organisation, family and of course aspects of yourself. Personal change management is all about being aware of your own emotions, being aware of the change process and where possible being aware of your emotions as you experience change. The likelihood is that when change occurs, you will first react to it emotionally and only later think more rationally about your experience.

8. Acknowledging personal values

Often it is not until we begin reflective practice that we begin to realise that we have certain values. For many, this is the first time these values have come to the fore. It is as if they have remained dormant for years in your subconscious.

TASK TASK **TASK** TASK **TASK** **TASK** TASK **TASK** TASK **TASK** **TASK** TASK

Think about where values come from.

It is like answering the nature/nurture question, and that answer is 'both'. You inherit some of your values, the others are learned from significant others in your life. These include your parents, relatives, teachers, and other influential people in your life. Values are also appropriated from experiences such as reading and watching the television. Values are shared within generations both in terms of your family and the broader term of 'generation' being those people who were born at around the same years as you. Other values are assumed from factors such as where you live. So your village, town or city will have a bearing on your values, as will the region and country in which you live. A characteristic of values is that they last a very long time. They are subject to change, depending on your life experiences but in general they are fairly constant.

When you reflect, sooner or later you are going to experience a clash of values. This has the potential to create a problem for you because your own personal values can clash with the values of your learners, peers or your organisation. Arguably some values are useful to us, while others are not, and these will only be made apparent as you make your own way through the various dilemmas which are sent your way as you reflect. What is important is to identify what your values actually are by doing this you will be more able to:

- realise that another person is not wrong, they just have different values;
- be able to see beyond what appears to be belligerent behaviour and realise their values are different;
- value the perspectives of others and not cause unintentional offence;
- be true to yourself.

What is important is not to judge your values or others by attributing a value to them. Instead it is better to become aware of your own values and be aware of and make allowances for others. People can and do feel very strongly about their values, which are often deeply embedded. They can be found in areas such as religion, cultural identity, tradition and within the unwritten protocols of everyday living.

However, we can generalise a person's values by considering the work of Thomas Harris. He suggested that we take one of four stances which influence our values and subsequently our behaviour. See the diagram below.

I'm OK You're OK	I'm OK You're not OK
I'm not OK You're OK	I'm not OK You're not OK

The above diagram indicates the four positions we can hold when judging the worth or value of another. You will notice that it is possible for a person to hold either a positive or negative value of themselves and others.

I'm OK, You're OK. Here a person accepts both their own and other people's values equally. This is the best situation and what you want to strive for.

I'm OK, You're not OK. In this instance you are right and the other person is wrong. This can be found in many areas such as, sexism, ageism, racism, etc.

I'm not OK You're OK. Here the person believes themselves to be generally unworthy and looks up to others. This is where a person is very insecure; this leads to dependency on others for direction and guidance.

I'm not OK, You're not OK. This is an unpleasant and unconstructive situation where an individual sees themselves and others without any merit.

It is worth stopping to think and to consider exactly how you are relating to the above on different occasions, bearing in mind the best place to be is 'I'm OK, You're OK'. This may not always be straightforward to achieve because your personal values drive your actions and reactions. Your values are closely aligned to your emotions and as a result you are quick to respond, judge and find fault in others. However, your values are your own, so your best policy is to keep them that way and be aware and accept that others have theirs.

9. Taking your own advice

Perhaps there is some truth in the saying that we only really listen to our own advice. Have you ever seen a person with an issue that is concerning them? Often they discuss that issue with a number of people. However, eventually they take advice offered from someone who agrees with what they were thinking in the first place. This person could have saved a lot of time because we don't require others to tell us what we already know.

People are generally critical of what they do in a negative way, for example they tend to dwell on what was done poorly as opposed to what they did well. If you engage in reflection you will be able to act upon your own uniquely informed criticism and improve what you do as a result. It is generally recognised that you are the most honest critic of your own work. The only person who knows exactly why you did what you did is you. For example, after an assessed lesson, when the assessor asks, *How do you feel that lesson went?*, you generally highlight the aspects of your lesson that did not go well in a way that if you were to receive that criticism from any other person, you could find their observations rude or at least very harsh. It appears to be human nature that we treat ourselves more harshly than others would treat us. If this is the case, perhaps we should consider how we can benefit from this situation. The first thing to do is to realise that when we are reacting to any given situation, our first reaction is to do this emotionally. Often this takes the form of self-doubt, which is not the most useful state of mind. Being honest with ourselves does not mean beating ourselves up. Instead, we are more likely to benefit by taking an objective approach by dealing with the facts. Only later when the emotional aspects have subsided can we take a more dispassionate and unemotional approach and consider what happened in more objective terms.

10. Recognising emancipatory benefits

Self-doubt is a normal state of mind for many who are new to teaching. This is because you are finding your way through what is new territory and you discover that you don't have the map. If you are lucky you have pieces of a map but they don't join together and you may not even be too sure if they are all a part of the same map. You find that you have many questions and very few answers. You are now recognising the existence of things that before you were not even aware of and perhaps may not have the words to accurately describe what is occurring. You may wonder if what you are doing is right in the circumstances, whether you were too soft or too harsh with a difficult learner, or whether you can answer the questions to the satisfaction of the students. No one said it would be easy, but you hadn't realised the challenges would be quite so great. Again, this is a normal state for the new teacher or a more experienced teacher in a new environment with new subjects to teach. Your aim is to make sense of your new environment, to see how it all fits together, what the unwritten rules are and where you fit into the picture. Hillier (2005, page 20) offers sound advice when she observes that, *By reflecting critically, instead of continuing with our feelings of self-doubt, that we are impostors in our classrooms, or that we are failing as teachers, racked with guilt, we can become positive in our search for new understandings of our practice and more ways to deal with the challenges that confront us continually*. She suggests that by doing this you take control over your professional practice in the knowledge that you cannot change everything but you accept that there are some things you can change. As a result the experience becomes what she describes as *emancipatory*; in other words, it liberates you.

Often just thinking about a situation can help you feel differently about something when you attempt to place things into context. Acknowledging that you are not personally responsible for every little thing and everybody can be a useful and enlightening experience for some. Realising that you don't know all there is to know and you don't have the questions, let alone the answers, and appreciating that you cannot be expected to know all there is to know at the drop of a hat unburdens you. Reflecting gives you the space to put things into perspective; it gives you time out to catch your breath and to take stock of what you are experiencing. It enables you to make sense of your own unique and individual world. Take for example the pieces of the map referred to earlier – bit by bit as you make sense of your new world, you gather new pieces of that map. Gradually the spaces are filled and you begin to appreciate the connections and relationships that exist. You start to understand how things go together and identify the most suitable way to get from one place to another. Your map can be three-dimensional, reflecting upon the many and varied aspects of your professional perspective. Remember, there is more to your professional practice than the classroom alone. For example, there are your colleagues to consider, the organisational rules (both written and otherwise), standard operating procedures, policies, politics, social norms, social groups, meetings, tutorials, committees, focus groups, training days and the outside agencies, to name but a few. As Warnke (in Hillier, 2005) observes, your position is informed by other positions. As a result you gradually begin to appreciate not only where you are but the nature and position of what surrounds you. Gradually you find and recognise your own place within the big picture; the map has now taken on the characteristics of a three-dimensional, colourful, moving film with surround sound!

TASK TASK **TASK** TASK **TASK** **TASK** TASK **TASK** TASK **TASK** **TASK** TASK

Look back at the benefits of reflective practice you identified for yourself earlier. Are they similar or different from the ones we identified? We encourage you to share your reflections by contacting our website QTLS.net.uk.

A SUMMARY OF **KEY POINTS**

In this chapter we have looked at the following key points:

> **Reasons for reflective practice. The first reason for engaging in reflective practice is maybe an 'extrinsic' one, as the IfL requires you to reflect on the CPD activities you have undertaken. To count towards the 30 hours (or pro-rata), you need to critically reflect on what you have learned; how you have applied this to your practice; and how it has impacted on your learners' experience and success.**

> The meaning of professionalism. The characteristics of professionalism include the setting of high standards; maintaining appropriate specialist knowledge; and shared values. The setting of high standards has been achieved with the introduction of the Further Education Teachers' Qualifications Regulations 2007; maintaining appropriate specialist knowledge by commitment to CPD; and shared values are achieved by adhering to the Code of Professional Practice and the associated disciplinary processes. Ultimately, professionalism leads to self-regulation.

> Recognise the link between learning and reflective practice. We have discussed the SOLO taxonomy: noticing, making sense, making meaning, working with meaning and transformative learning. From this we have argued that the more you reflect on your learning, the deeper it is. A surface approach to learning requires little reflection, a deep approach more.

> Ten benefits of reflective practice. The areas where reflective practice can be beneficial to you very much depend on your own personality and skills. They can be linked to your professional as well as to your personal life. We have highlighted benefits to your teaching practice; skills such as problem-solving, critical thinking and decision-making; organisational and personal change-management skills; your personal values; relying on your own advice, leading to emancipatory benefits.

REFERENCES AND FURTHER READING REFERENCES AND FURTHER READING

Armitage, A, Bryant, R, Dunhill, R, Hayes, D, Hudson, A, Kent, J, Lawe, S and Atherton, JS (2005) *Learning and teaching: SOLO taxonomy* www.learningandteaching.info/learning/solo.htm. Accessed: 6 February 2008.

Biggs, J and Collis, K (1982) *Evaluating the quality of learning: the SOLO taxonomy*. New York: Academic Press.

Bolton, G (2001) *Reflective practice*. Writing and professional development. London: Paul Chapman Publishing.

Elder, L and Paul, R (1994) Critical thinking: why we must transform our teaching. *Journal of Developmental Education*, www.accd.edu/sac/history/keller/ACCDitg/SSCT.htm.

Freidson, E (2001) *Professionalism: the third logic*. Cambridge: Polity Press.

Harris, TA (1970) I'm *OK–You're OK*. London and Sydney: Pan Books.

Harris, TA and Harris AB (1986) *Staying OK*. London: Pan Books.

Hillier, Y (2005) *Reflective teaching in further and adult education* (2nd edition). London: Continuum.

Institute for Learning (2007a) *Guidelines for your continuing professional development (CPD)*. Guidance document, October 2007.

Institute for Learning (2007b) *Inform*. Winter 2007.

Moon, J (2004) *A handbook of reflective and experiential learning theory and practice*. London: RoutledgeFalmer.

Osterman, KF and Kottkamp, RB (1993) *Reflective practice for educators. Improving schooling through professional development*. Thousand Oaks, CA: Sage.

Renwick, M (2003) *Teaching and training in post-compulsory education*. Maidenhead: Open University Press.

Robson, J (2006) *Teacher professionalism in further and higher education* London: Routledge.

Tummons, J (2007) *Becoming a professional tutor in the lifelong learning sector*. Exeter: Learning Matters.

Websites

teamtechnology.co.uk (Publishers of quality online articles and resources)
www.teamtechnology.co.uk/changemanagement.html.

3
Professional reflective practice
– the process

By the end of this chapter you will be able to:

- describe the four stages of professional reflective practice;
- explain the meaning of the five steps and the mnemonic SCOPE;
- explain the meaning of the mnemonic SHARK and 'exhaustive whys';
- relate your reflections to your professional practice by applying the process as described;
- design an action plan.

Professional Standards

This chapter relates to the following Professional Standards.

Professional Values:

AS 4 Reflection and evaluation of their own practice and their continuing professional development as teachers.

Professional Knowledge and Understanding:

AK 4.3 Ways to reflect, evaluate and use research to develop own practice, and to share good practice with others.

Professional Practice:

AP 4.2 Reflect on and demonstrate commitment to improvement of own personal and teaching skills through regular evaluation and use of feedback.

AP 4.3 Share good practice with others and engage in continuing professional development through reflection, evaluation and the appropriate use of research.

Introduction

As stated by Reece and Walker (2006, page 33) *experiences should be interspersed by periods of reflection*. This chapter describes the process of reflective practice, explaining what to do at each stage. A reminder of the four stages of professional reflective practice is shown below. Although it is cyclic in nature and you can begin at any stage, for ease we will start at Experience. As it is not always easy to decide which experience to focus on, the chapter suggests some techniques to get you started. To be able to reflect on the experience you need to analyse it and look at it from different perspectives. Again, this chapter offers some useful mnemonics and activities for you to try out. Next, you will link your experience to your professional practice and devise an action plan, taking you to your next experience.

Still stuck? A list at the end of the chapter of key words and ideas should be helpful.

Stage 1 of professional reflective practice – experience

It is not always easy to decide what is suitable as an example of an experience. You may feel that what has occurred may be mundane or not suitably different, or you may think that it lacks sufficient content. It is helpful to remember that what you are trying to achieve is to consider your experience and linking it to your professional practice and relevant theory. The experience can relate to many areas, not just your experiences of your teaching practice within the classroom. Until you give it a go, you are likely to remain unsure of what exactly to do. However, this is one of those situations where you can jump in at the deep end without the worry of getting it right first time. The process is uniquely personal to you and whatever you choose to reflect upon, will be right for you. Later, as you become more experienced, you will become more confident to embark on the process and perceptive in your choice of experience. Later still, when you have reflected on a number of situations or incidences, you may notice emerging patterns of behaviour or recognise similar end results to your actions. For example, you can make a conscious effort to identify why at the end of meetings you regularly end up with all the work, or you could question why it is that your relationship with some groups of students is better than with others.

Occasionally some people get stuck: they just cannot get started or think of an experience suitable for reflective practice. If this reflects how you feel, consider the list of possible situations, circumstances, experiences, etc., at the end of this chapter under the heading 'Getting stuck'. On the other hand, although you believe you recognise what may be a suitable topic for reflection, or even a critical incident (i.e. something of particular significance and worthy of further reflection), you may still be waiting for the first occurrence of that topic. The advice is not to wait for a particular topic, situation or incident to happen. Start reflecting on anything that has happened, regardless of its significance or immediate impact. The first steps are the most difficult, but once you start, it becomes much easier.

The five steps

Step 1

There are five general areas for you to consider when directing your thinking, just remember to SCOPE it:

- Social;
- Communicational;

- Organisational;
- Personal;
- Economic.

List what you think will fall into each of these categories.

Social

These are aspects of your professional practice involving your relationships with your students, peers, managers and other people you come into contact with inside and out of your organisation.

Communicational

Communicational issues include your ability to converse with others, write in various styles according to the task, convey thoughts, ideas and emotions, talk to various groups, exchange ideas, speak at an appropriate level, correspond via emails and reports, instruct individuals and groups and, most importantly, to listen.

Organisational

Here the emphasis of your thinking relates to the structure and characteristics of the organisation, the subject matter being delivered, the time afforded for marking, tutorials and general support. Your thinking can also consider the philosophy of the organisation; this is reflected in its general practices and the manner in which it deals with its employees and students.

Personal

This considers how you fit into the general scheme of things: your values, beliefs, feelings and behaviour. Think about your work–life balance for instance. What time do you need to be at your place of work, how long does it take you to get there, do you need childcare or other care arrangements? Do you teach evening classes, leaving you with your head still buzzing when it's time for bed? Do you feel confident and competent teaching the subject specialism to your students?

Economic

This examines the effect that money has upon your professional practice. It includes your salary (or hourly rate if you are a sessional teacher), overtime payments, expense claims or allowances and pension contributions. Furthermore, you could consider the resources available to support your teaching. Your classroom may have an interactive whiteboard or other ICT equipment. On the other hand, you may be teaching in the community with only a flipchart available. Does this have an impact on your students' learning experience? Are there implications for you? If you have an interactive whiteboard you may need training in how to use it; with only a flipchart you may feel restricted in the delivery of your lesson. Whatever your resources available in the classroom, up to date or basic, you can reflect on what you need or would like and how it affects your teaching and students' learning.

Your first step in the process is to select a general area for consideration from the SCOPE: Social, Communicational, Organisational, Personal, Economic.

Selecting a general area enables you to make your first choice. At this point you have not yet decided exactly what it is you wish to reflect upon but now you have made a start.

Step 2

Think about and list the three most memorable situations or incidents in relation to your selected SCOPE area:

1	
2	
3	

It doesn't matter if you can't see the significance of what you have chosen; the fact that you consider them the most memorable is a good thing because they obviously made an impact on you; there will be a reason for this even though you can't recognise it at this time.

Step 3

Situations or incidents fall into four distinct areas:

Positive and large	Positive and small
Negative and large	Negative and small

An example of each is provided below.

Positive and large For example, *I designed an e-learning package, intended to assist the new members of staff with their initiation process. This has now been formally adopted by the college.*

Negative and large For example, *The class consisted of students between the ages of 14 and 16, mostly male. They began to hum, very quietly at first and then louder and louder and all the time, they kept a straight face. I don't think I can deal with that class again; I didn't join the college to put up with this! I just don't know what to do.*

Positive and small For example, *I finished the lesson exactly on time.*

Negative and small For example, *I didn't realise that my claim form for my travelling expenses had to be in at a certain time. The admin unit has refused to forward the claim. I won't get my money refunded.*

Your chosen situation can be a positive or negative one. From the examples above, you can see that whatever you choose does not necessarily have to be big. A situation can be quite small and yet impact significantly on a person. Defining the example using the above criteria enables you to start to think about the situation.

Think about your examples and identify in which category yours fall.

1	2	3
Positive and large	Positive and large	Positive and large
Negative and large	Negative and large	Negative and large
Positive and small	Positive and small	Positive and small
Negative and small	Negative and small	Negative and small

Critical incidents

These situations or incidents are sometimes referred to as 'critical incidents'. A critical incident is any incident or situation which impacts on your professional practice. As a person engaging in professional reflective practice, you are aware that some situations will be highly significant. However, perhaps you have found nothing yet beyond the every-day normal, mundane activities that don't appear to lend themselves towards comment. You are aware of the existence of critical incidents, but as yet have not experienced one, so you wait and wait in the hope that something huge will hit you hard. But that is just the point: a critical incident will not jump out at you and grab you by the throat, the things that are termed critical incidents are those which appear at first to be just normal and mundane. Trip (1993, page 17) refers to these things as 'routines'. He suggests that these routines enable us to expose those issues that contain *the kind of questions about our practice which lead us to confront our professional values and judgements.*

At first your critical incidents may not be obvious to you until you start questioning the most familiar to you. These things are contained in your daily routines, the things you don't have to give conscious thought to. Tripp (1993, page 13) suggests that *while the strength of routines is that they enable us to do things without consciously attending to them, that is also their danger.* The danger here is that we will simply miss the significance of what we are doing without question.

Step 4

Ask yourself if you feel that the examples you have chosen lend themselves to further attention and consideration, in other words do they make an impact?

1	2	3
Yes	Yes	Yes
No	No	No

If they do not lend themselves to further attention and consideration, repeat steps 1 to 4 with the other general areas (SCOPE).

Step 5

Select the example that interests you the most.

By now you are well on your way to understanding the key characteristics of a situation or incident that will guide your thoughts in deciding which to choose. To summarise:

Step 1 Identify a general area from the mnemonic SCOPE.
Step 2 Choose three examples.

Step 3   Categorise the examples in terms of good/bad, positive/negative.
Step 4   Consider impact assessment.
Step 5   Select your example for the next stage (reflection).

TASK TASK **TASK** TASK **TASK** **TASK** TASK **TASK** TASK **TASK** **TASK** TASK

Select an example for reflection by using the SCOPE process.

Stage 2 of professional reflective practice – reflection

Having decided upon a suitable experience, whether it be a social, communicational, orga-nisational, personal or economic incident, the next thing to do is to record it. The structure of your writing is not necessarily important. You could, for example, just write down what happened as it enters your head on paper. Unfortunately the human brain does not remem-ber things chronologically and inevitably an important element may be subsequently remembered and then it will need to be included into your account in some way. If you use a computer this is not an issue as you can just insert the account wherever it is best situated.

If you structure your initial writing, then more can be gained from remembering an experi-ence. This is because the brain can fit the pieces together like a jigsaw puzzle. As the pieces link together, some parts of the picture becomes clearer, links can then be made between certain features and as a result a greater understanding of the overall picture is achieved. It all depends on your own preferences: some like to just get the words down and work on the screen; others prefer a more precise approach, with much of the structure and form having been worked out in advance. It is useful to recognise different ways of thinking. Knight (2002) suggests the following three: visual, auditory or feelings. She describes these as:

- *Visual* You think in pictures. You represent ideas, memory and imagination as mental images, e.g. a picture of a cup of coffee.
- *Auditory* You think in sounds. These sounds could be voices or noises, e.g. the sound of a coffee machine.
- *Feelings* You represent thoughts as feelings, either internal emotions or the thought of a physical touch. We will include taste and smell in this category of feelings, the taste of the coffee for example, or the aroma.

(Knight, 2002, page 17)

Being aware of the way in which you relate to the world may assist you to understand the way in which you think and communicate within yourself. When making sense of an incident or situation, you could find that as you think about what happened you see a film or a series of pictures in your mind's eye. Alternatively you may actually hear a discussion that took place between yourself and a colleague. Perhaps you can relate to the way in which the occurrence made you feel. It is likely that you experience a combination of these, but people generally have a preferred way of thinking. For example, if you identify that you are a visual thinker, then you can make a conscious effort to search for the finer detail or to look for the bigger picture. The auditory thinker may choose to identify whether the sounds heard are those of a voice, either your own or another's, or other sounds. The feelings thinker may be experiencing feelings of lightness or alternatively of pressure. These feelings may be located at particular parts of the body, a little like feelings of butterflies in your tummy or the tired heaviness of your legs. If you want to, you can choose a visual, auditory or feelings method of thinking other than your preferred method of thinking; this may help you to see things from a different perspective. What is important to remember is that the way in which you think is linked directly to the way in which you communicate to others.

The following techniques assist you as you recall your experiences: the SHARK mnemonic and the 'exhaustive whys'.

SHARK

The SHARK mnemonic guides your thinking so that you are more able to revisit the experience, focusing on differing elements of the same circumstances. It is described as:

S Saw;
H Heard;
A Action;
R Result;
K Knowledge.

Saw
Set the scene by describing what you saw, where you were, who else was present, the time of day, etc. Next consider what had happened, describe in detail what you observed and experienced, who did what, what someone else did. Try to be as detailed as possible as this will assist you later.

Heard
Describe what you heard, who said what, why you said and did what you did, why you chose not to say and do other things.

Action
Describe what you did next by way of the necessary action to deal with the situation. Don't confuse this with any actions that may have been a part of the situation. The action here refers to a course of action intended to rectify a situation, remedy a problem, reduce feelings of anger or change behaviour that enables another person to better understand another's position. How did this make you feel?

Result
As a result of your actions, what happened next? Did the situation change; was it a positive or negative outcome? Did the situation remain the same? What did you notice as a result of your intervention?

Knowledge
Thinking about what happened, how has your knowledge of this or similar situations changed? Why did it happen? How did it happen? Is it likely to happen again?

You will notice that an integral part of the writing process is reflection. As you write your account, following the SHARK mnemonic, you begin to think about what actually occurred. Using this structure enables you to identify the what, when, where, who and which of an experience. Furthermore, it will guide your thinking, taking you to considerations of why and how. Of these two questions it is arguably the question 'why' that is often the most enlightening.

Exhaustive whys

A useful technique here is to ask as many 'whys' as you can about a situation. Sometimes it is useful to ask the why of things about yourself, for example why you do things in a certain way or why you react to things in a particular way. Consider the following scenario. You share the delivery of a programme/course with a colleague. You do not teach at the same time, so you expect to keep in regular contact. Today you came to work expecting to discuss the previous session before delivering your lesson; however, your colleague has phoned the college stating that her car is playing up and that unfortunately she is going to be late. This is the fourth time in two weeks that her car has given her problems. You are cross.

The first question to ask is: *Why?*

Because she had taught the group yesterday and you expected to discuss their progress. *Why?*

Because you have to teach the group today and you needed to know what they had covered exactly. *Why?*

Because that is the done thing and it is professional and it is something that she never even considers and it gets on your nerves. *Why?*

Because she does no more than she has to, she appears not to care and you find it very annoying. *Why?*

Because it interferes with your ability to teach as effectively as possible and you consider her attitude and behaviour to be unacceptable. *Why?*

Because what she is doing conflicts with your personal values.

Arguably the exhaustive whys may be rather monotonous but they do help to get to the root cause of a situation. In this example, it enabled the thinker to realise that the underpinning problem was that of values and as a result possibly the expectations of others based on strongly held values. The exhaustive whys technique, although simple, is an effective method to begin to analyse a situation or incident. Sometimes we don't stop to think about the decisions we make, we are pulled in various directions by the needs of others and our own desires. Covey et al. (1995) refer to the struggle between the clock and the compass. The clock represents what we do with and how we manage our time, whereas the compass is representative of what we feel is important in our life and the direction in our life. Sometimes there is a struggle between the two. We may recognise this struggle but be unaware of exactly what the contributing factors are. Analysing a situation is important because unless we recognise the various aspects of a situation or incident, its influences and relationships, we cannot understand the significance of the experience. We cannot reflect unless we understand what it is we are reflecting upon.

Analysis

Analysis is the term used to describe something's essential features and the relationships between them. For example, if you were to analyse a car, you would need to consider its function. You could ask: is it sporty, comfortable, suited to carrying things, or designed to go off-road? To answer these questions, you need to look at the component parts. First, the outside of the car: it is a nice shade of blue and fairly large but not the most aerodynamic of shapes. It has four wheels, the tyres are not too chunky, it has a tow bar and lights. It even has roof bars. Inside the car you notice there are five seats which appear comfortable and removable. Then you discover another two seats, which are folded away. It has air condi-tioning, a CD player, an automatic gear selector, a steering wheel, two foot pedals and lots of information for the driver in the form of dials and coloured lights. Outside again and you look under the bonnet; there you notice a fuel-injected 2 litre petrol engine. The boot is roomy and suitable for lots of luggage or dogs.

You have now identified the essential features of this vehicle. If it helps, you can picture all the parts removed from the car's shell in bits on a garage floor. But there is more to analysis than identifying the essential features. The other part is to identify the relationships between these features. With a machine such as a car, this is relatively simple. You can communicate with the engine mostly with your feet via the accelerator pedal; the other pedal commu-nicates with the brakes, which are attached to the wheels; direction is obtained with the steering wheel; and the electrical system powers the lights and CD player. To make it all work, fuel is required and a road is desirable. You can see various functions that this car may be able to deal with: the seats are removable, which turns it into a small van if required and the tow bar and the roof bars mean that this car is practical when necessary. Your analysis has led you to understand that you are looking at a multi-purpose vehicle (MPV).

In the world of people, identifying the relationships between things can be trickier. The study of social science, which is the study of human aspects of the world, is not always a simple task. Often the relationships between one thing and another are hidden, camouflaged to a degree and are frequently multi-layered. Your aim as a professional reflective practitioner is to attempt to make sense of a very mixed up and confusing world, and the task is further compounded by the fact that those around you may have no idea what is happening in their world either.

Your reflections are an attempt to make sense of the situations or incidents you encounter in your professional capacity. As you reflect, you may notice more about yourself, your teach-ing, other people, your own institution, other institutions and the government. This is because quite simply you are being bothered to stop and look around you while others around you rush off down the road, head down, MP3 playing at max volume.

Having taken the time to look, you then think about what you have noticed and having done that you attempt to identify informed links. In other words, you try to make sense of your world and see how it fits in with the numerous others' worlds. You may come to realise that nothing is actually as you first thought it to be.

TASK TASK **TASK** TASK **TASK** **TASK** TASK **TASK** TASK **TASK** **TASK** TASK

Using the example identified in the previous task, consider the different aspects of the experience; what is its root?

Stage 3 of professional reflective practice – professional practice

The next stage in the cycle is to have some method of evaluating the experience. Evaluating the experience serves to focus your thoughts and provides a natural boundary. By now you will have identified one or more situations or incidents and analysed them. To evaluate your experience, more questions can be asked.

How does it relate to my professional practice?

There are many aspects of your professional practice that could be influenced from one experience. If during your reflections you have identified a need to be more assertive, this can influence many aspects of your professional practice, within the SCOPE range. Specific examples of you not being assertive could include: the willingness to take on new tasks even though you are much too busy as it is; the inability to say no to a student who asks for you to have a 'quick look' at their work for the fifth time that week, or dealing with emails from your students on a Sunday evening because you don't have the time to deal with them at work.

How does this relate to me?

In the example above, your lack of assertiveness relates to you in terms of time management and work overload. Taking on too many activities will leave you no time for your core role, for example, that of lesson planning and teaching, and may leave you in a state of burnout or exhaustion.

What did I like, or not like, and why?

Having come to the conclusion that you are not assertive, the question of what you don't like may be expressed in very general terms, such as the feeling of being taken for granted or not being appreciated after having spent so much time helping others.

What will I do differently as a result of this?

As a result of your reflective practice you may be reluctant to take on new tasks but instead negotiate with your line manager a more even division of tasks within an agreed timeframe; the ability to say no to a student who is very demanding by cultivating a more independent approach to their learning by promoting critical analysis of their own work; or to realise that there is only so much time in one day and dealing with emails from your students on a Sunday evening is perhaps not appropriate.

Am I being objective or subjective?

An objective approach is that of reacting to a situation by looking at the bare facts and basing an argument upon them, whereas a subjective approach is reacting to a situation in terms of feelings which may lack any form of evidence. It is not always easy to identify where we are coming from at first because rarely are the two nicely separated. Our experiences are a mix of objective and subjective issues. To make a credible argument, expressing yourself purely subjectively will not help your case. It is far better to refer to the evidence and then explain how that makes you feel.

Am I being positive or negative?

When practising professional reflective practice there is a tendency to 'plom' (De Board,1998, page 66) – 'Poor Little Old Me'. In other words, it is used as a platform to pour your heart out, attend confession or feel sorry for yourself. Low self-esteem and stress can contribute to this tendency. Be warned: it can happen to you, so to prevent this from happening, be aware of the positive or negative aspect of your writing. If you do feel that you have a tendency to view everything negatively, then for each negative entry, ensure your next entry is positive.

Why is this?

Looking at your working environment, institution, place of work, etc., ask yourself why what is happening is happening. Is it something you are doing, or not doing, the reason for the situation or incident under consideration, or is it something out of your control? What can you do to change things? What may be a consequence of that change? Do you still want that change?

What did I learn?

This considers what you know now compared with what you knew before. Learning is not a linear phenomenon: when we learn it can affect many aspects of the way in which we think about things; when we learn we change as a result. We can learn from our reflections, link this learning to our professional practice and then consolidate this as we decide on a suitable action plan.

Stage 4 of professional reflective practice – action plan

The final part of the cycle involves your action plan; this normally takes the form of specific goals. These goals are derived from considerations of your professional practice. Aim to make your goals SMART. In other words, they should be:

S Specific;
M Measurable;
A Achievable;
R Relevant;
T Time-bound.

Staying with the theme of assertiveness, the action plan may look a little like the following.

Action plan

Specific
To become more assertive.

Measurable
To reduce the time spent in unpaid work activity by 50 per cent and to do no work on Sundays.

Achievable

To attend an assertiveness course and be committed to personal change.

Relevant

If I don't do this I will burn out and be of no use to my students, myself or the organisation.

Time-bound

I have enrolled on the course which starts next week and runs for at total of ten weeks. By the end of this course I will achieve my goal.

TASK TASK **TASK** TASK **TASK** **TASK** TASK **TASK** TASK **TASK** **TASK** TASK

Draw up an action plan from the example you identified in the task for reflection using the SCOPE process.

An action plan can appear however you wish it to; it is entirely your choice. This example uses a SMART structure to assist with the concept. Other formats are offered later in this book. Having set an action plan and recorded it, you will be more likely to achieve that goal as opposed to just mulling it over as being a good idea. You can have as many goals on the go at one time as you wish, but be realistic. Some goals can be long term, others quite short. It is recommended that you identify a number of the shorter goals, as too many longer-term ones may make you feel as though you are not achieving as best you can. When you have achieved your goals you are then ready for the next experience, and so on.

Getting stuck

Occasionally you may get stuck, not knowing where or how to start. To support you, consider the following list of possible situations, circumstances, experiences, etc., under the headings: relationships, communication, subject matter, time, study and resources. Although typical of the subjects suitable for professional reflective practice, they represent only a fraction of topics for consideration.

Relationships (social considerations *SCOPE*)

Your relationship with the following (in no particular order).

- People you work with: peers, colleagues, reception staff, marketing department, catering staff, security staff, caretaker, the principal, vice/assistant principal, your mentor, head of department, head of school, classroom assistants, learning support assistants, human resources department, learning resource centre staff.
- Your learners: students in general, those with specific learning needs (including 'gifted' learners), those who don't want to be there, those who take drugs, very keen students, non-attendees, 'needy' or demanding students.
- External contacts: external verifiers, awarding bodies, partner/network colleges, employers, parents, pushy parents, absent parents.

Communication (communicational considerations SC*O*PE)

Your ability to communicate with others verbally, your ability to communicate as you recognise that your pronounced accent may impede communication, your written communication, your use of IT to communicate, your writing on the whiteboard, your spelling, your report writing, your listening skills, your active listening skills, your phone technique, your handwriting, your non-verbal communications, your interpersonal skills, dealing with younger people, dealing with older people, communication with ethnic minority groups, communicating your ideas, communicating instructions and communicating in sign language.

Subject matter (organisational considerations SCO*P*E)

Your knowledge of the subject, how it relates to you, how it relates to the students, how it relates to the overall course, how to sell it to the students, whether your knowledge is up to date, the level of the students' knowledge, the way you are going to teach the subject, how others normally teach it, the availability of suitable lesson plans, the existence of a scheme of work, how you have been told to teach it, how you would like to teach it, the amount of time given to the subject, the amount of time you would prefer to have, the depth of knowledge appropriate for this group, the depth of knowledge necessary for the course, matters of assessment, evaluation of the course, etc.

Time (again organisational considerations SCO*P*E)

Time you spend, in the classroom, in the office, on the phone, writing emails, looking at part-completed assignments, marking assignments, in tutorials, researching topics, preparing lessons, in meetings, at formal events, travelling to and from work, writing lesson plans, improving aims and objectives, writing schemes of work, supporting students, counselling students, coaching students, taking work home, working at the computer, inputting marks into a spreadsheet, designing innovative lessons, changing your practices, dealing with issues other than in your job description, time off, time allocated to your children, time allocated to your partner, time management, time wasted, time to study, time lost, making time, etc.

Study (personal considerations SCO*P*E)

Issues around the topic of your own personal study can include attending classes, your perceived ability, your readiness to study, the amount of time away from study, your ability to read, your understanding of a subject, difficulties with a topic, support from your teacher, feedback, being able to read the feedback, being treated like a valued person, having your contributions valued in class, access to the library, availability of books, the cost of new books, the cost of library fines, the helpfulness of the librarians, the ease of finding books, computerised systems, the willingness to learn, obstacles to your study, your attitude towards study, others' attitudes towards study, time for study, stolen time for study, study and the weather, study groups, peer support, those who share ideas, those who steal ideas, your own organisation of study, your attitude towards study, underlying intrinsic/extrinsic motivational factors influencing study.

Resources (economic considerations SCOP*E*)

Your ability to deal with a computer, Windows, Word, PowerPoint, Excel, an Apple Mac, your classroom, the seating, the lighting, the temperature, access to equipment, paperwork to complete to obtain equipment, operating the equipment, use of the internet, use of the intranet, use of email, access to the printer, use of the photocopier, using a memory pen, the standard of handouts, accessibility of resources, a whiteboard duster, cleaning fluid for the whiteboard, whiteboard pens, an interactive whiteboard, the blinds in your classroom, the blinds in your office, the level of heating, the effectiveness of the air-conditioning unit, access to fans, etc.

The above ideas are presented to enable you to broaden your perspective on what there is to reflect upon. They are presented here in a very ad hoc way, but nevertheless demonstrate the rich variations within a given subject, some of which may be very mundane but no less appropriate for consideration.

A SUMMARY OF **KEY POINTS**

This chapter has looked at the following key points.

> A description of each of the four stages of professional reflective practice.

> General areas to consider for reflection have been identified in the form of the mnemonic SCOPE. When directing your thinking, SCOPE it, in other words, consider the social, communication, organisational, personal and economic aspects.

> Techniques to guide your thinking, so that you can revisit an experience focusing on different elements are explained by the mnemonic SHARK (saw, heard, action, result, knowledge). The 'exhaustive whys' technique may help you to get to the root of situations, perhaps a repetitive but nevertheless a useful tool.

> By applying the process as described, evaluating your experience, you will be able to relate your reflections to your professional practice.

> The final part of the cycle involves an action plan with SMART goals derived from your professional practice.

> Finally, if you're still getting stuck, not knowing what to reflect on or write about, this chapter gives you some key ideas to focus on.

REFERENCES AND FURTHER READING REFERENCES AND FURTHER READING

Bolton, G (2005) *Reflective practice: writing and professional development* (2nd edition). London: Sage.

Calderhead, J and Gates, P (1993) *Conceptualising reflection in teacher development.* London: Falmer Press.

Covey, SR, Merril, AR and Merril, RR (1995) *First things first.* New York: Fireside.

De Board, R (1998) *Counselling for toads: a psychological adventure.* London: Routledge.

Knight, S (2002) *NLP at work. Neuro linguistic programming. The difference that makes a difference in business* (2nd edition). London: Nicholas Brearly.

Moon, J (1999) *Reflection in learning and professional development.* London: Kogan Page.

Moon, J (2004) *A handbook of reflective and experiential learning.* London: RoutledgeFalmer.

Reece, I and Walker, S (2006) *Teaching, training and learning; a practical guide.* Tyne and Wear: Business Education Publishers.

Tripp, D (1993) *Critical incidents in teaching. Developing professional judgement.* London: Routledge.

Websites

Quality Improvement Agency. Gold Dust resources. Reflective practice.
   http://excellence.qia.org.uk/GoldDust/reflectivepractice/reflective.html
The Westminster Partnership. Resources to support teaching reflective practice on initial teacher training programmes in the learning and skills sector.
   http://thewestminsterpartnershipcett.org.uk/

4
A psycholateral approach to professional reflective practice

By the end of this chapter you will be able to:

- describe the term 'psycholateral approach to professional reflective practice';
- recognise the three domains within education and learning;
- explain what is meant by thinking about thinking, relationships and organisational performance;
- explain the meaning of the terms, personal filters, levels of awareness and levels of competence;
- use techniques such as Johari window, Batari's box and the empty chair technique;
- conduct SWOT and performance needs analysis;
- relate your reflections to your professional practice by applying the techniques and models as described.

Professional Standards

This chapter relates to the following Professional Standards.

Professional Values:

AS 4 Reflection and evaluation of their own practice and their continuing professional development as teachers.

Professional Knowledge and Understanding:

AK 4.3 Ways to reflect, evaluate and use research to develop own practice, and to share good practice with others.

Professional Practice:

AP 4.2 Reflect on and demonstrate commitment to improvement of own personal and teaching skills through regular evaluation and use of feedback.

AP 4.3 Share good practice with others and engage in continuing professional development through reflection, evaluation and the appropriate use of research.

Introduction

Within this chapter you will be offered a variety of practical techniques and models to assist you with various aspects of the professional reflective practice cycle. The term 'psycholateral' is explained and various techniques and models are offered to enable you to practise professional reflective practice. By engaging in the activities offered, you will be given the opportunity to learn more about yourself, your likes, dislikes, how you react within certain situations, how people react to you, what works in social/organisational situations and what does not. The techniques and strategies suitable for the advancement of professional reflective practice are listed under the following titles, 'Thinking about thinking', 'Thinking about relationships' and 'Thinking about organisational performance'. Thinking about thinking considers some techniques available to you to enable you to recognise how you relate to and how you view your world. It is all about the relationship with yourself and how you go about making sense of your world. Before we understand other people, it is helpful to be able to understand ourselves. To do this we consider the following concepts.

Thinking about thinking

- Personal filters.
- Levels of awareness.
- Levels of competence.

Having given some thought to our own thinking, we next consider how we interact with others, and the following models are identified.

Thinking about relationships

- Johari window.
- Batari's box.
- Empty chair technique.

Having thought about ourselves and our relationships, lastly our situation is considered in terms of the context. Often a situation occurs as a combination of us, another and the organisational influences. Here the following are considered.

Thinking about organisational performance

- SWOT analysis.
- Performance needs analysis.

A psycholateral approach

The term 'psycholateral' has been chosen here to describe a particular approach to professional reflective practice, where a variety of thinking skills, techniques and strategies can be called upon to assist you. A psycholateral approach includes both the psychological approach to thinking, which pertains to the mind in terms of awareness, motivation, thoughts and feelings, and a lateral approach, which considers the many options available to the thinker at any given time. These options include consideration of theoretical models and approaches to thinking available to the professional reflective practitioner. A psycholateral approach provides an informed method of thinking, enabling you to consider any given incident or situation from a variety of perspectives and contexts, before arriving at a conclusion and importantly before deciding on any course of action.

As you contemplate your development, it is useful to think about your professional practice in terms of the three domains within education and learning, namely cognitive (thinking), psychomotor (skills) and affective (attitude). Within the cognitive domain, it will be fairly obvious to you what you know and what you need to find out. Equally, if your psychomotor skills are found wanting then you can practise whatever skill you wish to become proficient in until you are competent. The problems for you are most likely to occur within the affective domain. Here we are dealing with feelings, attitudes and behaviours, our own and others'. Some of the most demanding situations you will deal with will be psychological and sociological; in other words, how you relate to the world as an individual and how you relate to others and in turn they to you.

It is useful to consider some techniques and models to assist your understanding of how and why you sometimes end up in a situation without realising how you got there. On the other hand, you may wonder why nothing seems worthy of consideration for reflecting upon or having observed something you believe to be significant you are unsure what to do about it. When undertaking professional reflective practice, you will inevitably reach situations when you are unsure of what to do next. Sometimes during the reflecting stage of the process you may simply get stuck, or may recognise that things are happening but you may not have a full understanding of what is occurring. The following techniques and strategies are offered to help you through some of the more difficult and lonely moments as you consider what has actually happened and what you should do next. Different situations require different techniques or approaches to deal with them. For example, you may be experiencing thoughts where you feel that you can't think of anything that is worth reflecting upon, that nothing has happened of significance that is worth reflecting about and you are stuck. The following techniques and strategies lend themselves to use often during the reflection stage within the professional reflective practice model. This is because during the reflection stage you are able to ponder upon the nature, size, shape, meaning, significance and implications of an incident or situation. It is not until you have thought about a situation from many perspectives that you can begin to recognise the significance of that situation.

A psycholateral approach to reflective practice comprises of three stages. The first stage is to identify what techniques and strategies are available to you to inform and advance your professional reflective practice. Next the techniques and strategies are practised in various appropriate situations. Here you practise the techniques and strategies in order to increase your understanding of yourself, other people and the various situations in which you find yourself. Finally, over time, the techniques and strategies are internalised by you and are used as a matter of course almost instinctively.

Thinking about thinking

Personal filters

We are constantly bombarded with information in the form of sounds, visual images, smells of food and drink, and general distractions of one sort or another. If we are busy doing something, we tend to filter out these distractions. As you read this book, you will have filtered much of the information that is available to you. As you read, you will be made aware of some of these, for example if you are inside a building, the noise from other people inside, the noise outside; traffic, birds, sirens, perhaps road works. If you are sitting, it may be necessary to move as you become uncomfortable in the same position for any time. At that time you will become more aware of the feelings of your body. We have a personal filter through which we categorise information from the outside world. We constantly separate out sensory data, because if we did not, we would be inundated with so much information that we would be unable to function effectively. The act of filtering means that we are programmed to accept some information, but more importantly we dismiss that which we are programmed to consider not relevant. Fortunately, this process is managed for us by our unconscious mind and we don't have to give it any conscious thought. This means that our thoughts are not restricted to consider all the incoming information all the time, and instead we are free to occupy ourselves with the things that appear important to our conscious mind at any particular time.

Our personal filters are influenced by the context in which we find ourselves. For example, you may be aware of what is sometimes referred to as the cocktail party effect. This can occur where you have attended a social function and in the noisy environment you have picked up the fact that your name has been mentioned. You heard your name spoken even though at least half of the people in the room were talking, some quite loudly. You heard it even though the person speaking was on the other side of the room and not talking particularly loudly. You brain filtered all the other information and presented you with something that may have been of use to you.

Arguably, our personal filters serve a very useful purpose. They enable us to function when bombarded with information, provide an early warning system for danger and keep us focused upon danger when it occurs. Our personal filters perform one of three functions: they can delete, simplify or generalise information. What is actually deleted, simplified or generalised depends on the nature of your personal filters. When deleting information it is ignored completely. Your unconscious mind does not even bother you with it For example *The large stray dog on the other side of the road will probably stay on the road and present no danger to you; for the moment*. When simplifying, your unconscious mind makes it easy for you to understand, it doesn't bother with the ins and outs, you are just given the bare necessities. For example, *Move fast now!* Not, *There is a chance that that dog will continue running towards you snarling and barking. It would be a good thing to go into the nearest shop and close the door very quickly*. Generalising is more of an impression of something as it is unlikely that the subconscious mind actually thinks in words. But to give you an idea: *Big fast hairy crocodile thing – running – meet you – bite – hurt – go away fast!* It's more like experiencing a feeling than listening to advice. If you find yourself running away from danger, all of a sudden you find yourself running very quickly away from a situation, person, animal, etc. If you think about that experience, you will probably remember that you found yourself running before you have actually given yourself the time to weigh up the situation and apply some rational thought to what was going on. You may recognise this as the 'fight–flight' syndrome. As you recall such an incident, it is unlikely that you were consulted in the decision-making process. We remember flight–fight situations due to their intensity of emotion.

Our personal filters affect the way in which we think about things. Some things we give a lot of thought to before we act. However, there are possibly many things we give no conscious thought to; we just react to a situation. It would appear that we have little say on what information is actually filtered for us. It is a bit like a sliding scale: at one end we are only just aware of things, almost subconsciously, and at the other we focus all our concentration on a small number of things. The problem we face is that we can be unaware of the subtle way in which personal filters direct our behaviour, because we have no say in the process. We don't know even know what has been filtered out for us. Possibly we are aware of things because our personal filters have allowed us to be.

Arguably awareness is tempered by familiarity to a situation, environment, task, object or person. For the purpose of professional reflective practice, we may become less aware of the familiar, the mundane or those situations which are repeated frequently. We can respond to a situation in a semi-automatic manner. At this level of awareness we are in danger of missing the subtleties that underlie situations which could be suitable for professional reflective practice as the fine points of a situation are not immediately obvious to us. Whether or not you can affect the influence of your personal filters is a moot point. What professional reflective practice will do is enable you to question the legitimacy of your level of awareness and attentiveness. It will enable you to question your assumptions in relation to a situation or incident which are influenced by your own unique perception and, as a consequence, understanding.

TASK TASK **TASK** TASK **TASK TASK** TASK **TASK** TASK **TASK TASK** TASK

Think about your own filter at this moment and listen to your surroundings. What are you aware of now that you may have previously filtered out?

Levels of awareness

We offer three levels of awareness by way of illustration, primal, emotional and cognitive awareness. Although these are presented in the form of a hierarchy, it is acknowledged that an individual's level of awareness may differ from subject to subject and from situation to situation.

Primal awareness

At the most basic level, primal awareness you pay very little attention to whatever is occurring around you, your attention is focused very much in the here and now and is concerned with your own comfort and well-being. At this level you accept many things without question. Any thought that is given to others is formed in terms of how they may affect your own welfare. Although primal awareness acknowledges the presence of other people, situations, or the environment, etc., at this level you generally accept things as they are without question. In its simplest form primal awareness is pre-verbal; this means that thoughts are not formed as a result of thinking using words for expression and in any case little, if any, thought is given to things. It is also often pre-cognitive in the sense that it relies on a reaction to events as opposed to any considered action. Further, it embodies your most basic values and sense of self – your own well-being is considered before all else.

How does this relate to professional reflective practice? You may identify elements of this in yourself, work colleagues or your students. There are some subjects, incidents or situations that you choose simply to acknowledge or accept, no more than that. It could be that you have no interest in them or that you are too busy doing other things. On the other hand, you may feel ill or emotionally inclined not to pay attention to events that would otherwise interest you. Without wishing to stereotype, this level of awareness can sometimes be observed in teenagers whose self-obsession and ability to sleep for exceptionally long periods of time is staggering. At this level a person generally accepts things as they are: they don't question the underlying reasons for any event. Either they accept that a particular subject may exist but have no interest in finding out anything further about it. On the other hand, they may have no knowledge that the subject matter exists at all.

The advantages of this level of awareness are that there are few distractions from whatever you are doing; this is because you choose to ignore most things unless they impact upon you directly and at that moment. Ignorance is bliss. On the other hand the disadvantages are that you are in danger of missing out: a closed and unenquiring mind is not useful for furthering an education.

Emotional awareness

Second is emotional awareness, where your awareness triggers a response by way of a reaction to the people, situations and the environment at an emotional level. At this level the awareness is closely related to your feelings, and as a consequence emotional awareness can be reactive in nature. A person's awareness at this level confines their thoughts to view the world in a judgemental way, they are not taking the time to think about what they are doing or why they are doing it. It is not uncommon for people to exhibit a bipolar attitude to any given situation by identifying something in terms of being either good or bad; here there are no shades of grey.

This relates to professional reflective practice where an individual is functioning at an emotional level, which can be exhibited positively or negatively. Positively where a person engages in an activity in the belief that it is worthy of their attention and effort or not, as the case may be for a negative approach. The advantages include enthusiasm for a subject that can be engendered if you feel that the subject is worthy. Emotional awareness can be observed during periods of change where you are inclined to give value to what is occurring in terms of whether you agree or disagree with the proposed changes or whether you like or dislike the changes. It is also evident at a social level within a class where an 'us and them' situation may appear to exist.

Being in touch with your emotions means that you are unlikely to engage in an activity against your will. In other words, a lack of thinking through the subject fully does not enable you to see that by doing something you dislike at the time may reap rewards later. Further disadvantages include feeling that a subject is of no benefit to you but not knowing or being able to explain why. On occasion there may be a tendency to react from an emotional stance which may not always be appropriate. Reactions here are often limited to the fight–flight response. Here our assessment of a situation may be either to argue about something or to withdraw; both of these options may offer no rational explanation in considered hindsight.

Cognitive awareness

Third is cognitive awareness, where a person considers the world from a more informed basis. This is achieved not by relying on emotions to inform action, but by critically consider-ing and analysing information to make sense of the world. This is not to say that an emotional reaction does not take place, they do, but such a response is tempered by engaging in cognitive thought. At this level of awareness a person is able to question exactly why things are as they are. For example, they may take the time to consider the reasons behind the actions of others in an attempt to make sense of a particular situation. At this level people attempt to identify the problems that exist for themselves and others; they search for appropriate solutions and do their best to resolve them. They no longer consider things in terms of being simply right or wrong and can identify situations at the many levels in which they are situated; for people at this level, nothing is seen in terms of black and white, everything is a shade of grey.

How does this relate to professional reflective practice? In general a deeper insight is anticipated at this level due to the effect of thinking cognitively rather than emotionally. For example, in order to fully understand a subject, it may be necessary to think around the subject, perhaps read around the subject matter or consider a similar incident or to discuss the various aspects of the situation or issues with others.

The advantages of cognitive awareness are many and varied. Awareness at this level will ensure that all aspects of a situation are explored and the links between them are recognised. The result of taking the time and effort to consider the complexities and possibilities of any situation, at many levels, implies that success is more probable. As success builds upon success you can experience a form of self-fulfilling prophesy where new insights and possibilities are presented. The disadvantages could include what is sometimes coined 'paralysis of analysis', where too much thinking around a subject means that you do not know when to stop thinking about something and nothing useful actually gets done.

There is though an important aspect associated with any level of awareness and one that mutes ability and extinguishes talent, because it is dependent upon a positive emotional attitude. An inappropriate, negative or bad attitude towards any situation, person or organisation will ensure disappointment. It is very difficult to employ professional reflective practice at this level of awareness if your heart is not in it, as such any attempt at progress is doomed to failure.

The implications for you as a professional reflective practitioner

As a professional reflective practitioner, you may identify these three levels of awareness in yourself and those around you. This could impact on your teaching practice or perhaps you notice these characteristics in your work colleagues. A person's awareness at any one of these three levels will have a direct impact upon how they view their individual world. You can exhibit awareness at any one of these three levels. For example, it may be that you have no thoughts on a particular subject. You have such little interest that you simply could not care less either way; further, you don't care that you don't know.

At the level of primal awareness attention to detail is inhibited; in fact even attention to the bigger picture is lost. It is highly unlikely that professional reflective practice will be attempted in any form in relation to this particular subject by this type of person. However, other subjects may engender greater enthusiasm. On the other hand, you as an observer can perhaps use this information to inform your teaching practice or gain a better understanding of your relationships with your work colleagues. The level of awareness present is directly linked to a person's attitude. The challenge for the professional reflective practitioner when dealing with people functioning at the level of primal awareness, or if you are a member of this group in certain areas, is that of engendering motivation. It is difficult to engender a positive outlook and create an environment suitable for constructive engagement at this level.

At the level of emotional awareness people are more likely and able to display behaviours or communicate ideas that could irritate others. Unless tempered, the judgemental attitudes typical at this level are likely to offend or be expressed in over-generalised terms. From the point of view of the professional reflective practitioner, this can be an interesting encounter and again not without its challenges. These can include developing strategies for honest communication, introducing the concept of reflective practice and creating situations or discussions where positions are considered not in terms of the bipolar black and white but in terms of shades of grey.

Cognitive awareness enables people to act only after thinking about what they are doing. Unfortunately this is not always the case where often a person's first response is emotional. Awareness at this level enables people to temper this first reaction with an appropriate and considered response. Here a person is presented more options; this is achieved by considering their actions to any given situation. For example, during a heated discussion they can decide whether to wait to see what happens next, take the lead, keep quiet, look for support, argue their point, etc. In comparison, the person at the emotional level will have either run away or be rolling around on the floor fighting; but don't worry, the person at the primal level is still safely tucked up in bed. The professional reflective practitioner can be aware of the more complex reactions exhibited at the cognitive level and as a consequence consider their own reaction to others' actions.

TASK TASK **TASK** TASK **TASK** **TASK** TASK **TASK** TASK **TASK** **TASK** TASK

Think about your students, friends or relatives. Can you find an example of a person who exhibits the characteristics of each of the above levels?

Levels of competence

A model relating to incremental ability is that often attributed to Herzberg and is referred to as Herzberg's steps: although whether or not he was responsible for this is a matter of debate.

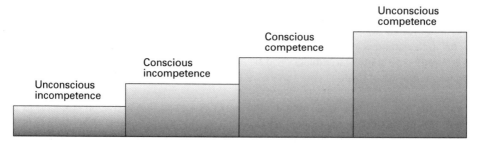

Here four levels of competence are identified, from unconscious incompetence to unconscious competence. The driving analogy is useful to explain this.

Unconscious incompetence

Before a person has attempted to drive a car, they have little idea of what is required of them. They are not able to drive, and further, have no concept of the various skills necessary to do so. Because they have no concept of what is involved with controlling the car in any way they cannot consider it and are described as being at the first step, that of unconscious incompetence.

Conscious incompetence

As they begin their lessons they start to realise that certain aspects of their driving require practice and perhaps it is not quite as easy as it first appeared to synchronise the accelerator and the clutch when pulling away. At this stage they have reached the next step, conscious incompetence.

Conscious competence

After a while they may have passed their driving test and have a green 'P' on the back of the car. They are driving quite well, but still have to think about what they are doing. Conversation or music in the car may be a form of distraction to them. Here they have reached the next step, conscious competence.

Unconscious competence

A few years down the line and they are driving well, in fact now they can listen to music or hold a conversation without being distracted from their driving. They have reached the last step of being unconsciously competent.

The implications for you as a professional reflective practitioner

As you strive to improve continuously, sometimes it helps to view your progress not in terms of how you did in relation to others, or how you did in relation to the prescribed competencies. Instead you can compare how you are doing to how you did previously; this form of assessment is referred to as ipsative, which derives from the Latin meaning 'of the self'.

When you partake in reflective practice, ask yourself which of the steps above apply to you. Are you at the same stage within each area of your professional practice?

Some of these areas you could consider are your skills such as:

- teaching practice;
- communications;
- negotiating;
- writing;
- organising;
- networking.

Obviously the list can be adapted to meet your individual circumstances. What is significant about the steps is that they enable you to identify your own ability in terms that mean something personally to you. There is no definition of competence within this model, it is a personal thing; you decide. Arguably, the most important step is between unconscious incompetence and conscious incompetence, where there is a realisation that something exists and as a consequence you will have to work towards improving in that area.

TASK TASK **TASK** TASK **TASK** **TASK** TASK **TASK** TASK **TASK** **TASK** TASK

Think about where you are in terms of the steps in relation to some situations at work at home or at college. What is it that makes the difference in you? How do you know when you have moved from one step to the next? Can you move back down the steps?

Thinking about relationships

Johari window

	Known to self	Not known to self
Known to others	1 Open	2 Blind
Not known to others	3 Hidden	4 Unknown

Johari window was named after its authors Joseph Luft and Harry Ingham by combining their first names. It is a model used to indicate aspects of human interaction and self-awareness. The word 'model' is used to describe a simplified representation of an idea or concept. Each window represents a feature of personal awareness about us and is described in terms of what is known to us, about ourselves, and what is known to others. According to Luft (1969, page 13) *The four quadrants represent the total person in relation to other persons*.

1. The Open window represents things that you know about yourself and that others know about you also. For example, this can be knowledge of your name, age, where you live, what you do for a living, likes and dislikes, friends, social status, religion, etc. In essence it is anything about you which is characteristic of you. In this model, the windows can be large or small. This is because when a person first gets to know you, the Open window will be very small for them (you of course know lots about yourself). As you divulge more to the other person, the window gets larger as they get to know more about you.

2. The Blind window represents things that the other person knows about you about which you are unaware. An example of this is when one is oblivious to the fact that their make-up has smudged, but the person observing can see this factor. The window can represent things such as aspects about your personality about which you are unaware, such as the fact that you have a tendency to avoid some topics of conversation and attempt to introduce others, or that you crave attention and have a tendency to do things to steal attention. If the other person discusses the issue of attention-seeking with you, then the second, Blind, window becomes smaller and as a result the first window becomes larger.

3. The Hidden window represents things that you know about yourself but that you hide or choose not to divulge to others. We are cautious with other people in the belief that self-disclosure could lead to us being teased or ridiculed or that we could lose our social standing as a result. Different people are presented various amounts of disclosure. For example, our life partner will generally know far more about us than our boss and our doctor may be privy to certain aspects of our lifestyle or habits. Again, if we choose to divulge information to another person, the Open window enlarges.

4. The Unknown window contains information that neither you nor the other person is aware of. Working on new projects or groups of people enables us to realise aspects of ourselves about which we had previously no idea. For example, sometimes you do not know how you are going to react to a situation until you find yourself there.

This model is a lot about the process of socialisation and the contract we embark on when socialising with others. Here one person chooses to disclose something about themselves and in return they expect the other to disclose something. This process continues with the two Johari windows changing in size as more is revealed about each other. This continues until the time one person discloses and the other is unwilling to reciprocate and the contract stops; or when both agree not to enter into conversation about one of the more potentially thorny topics of conversation. In an ideal world, the Johari window would appear with the Open window being largest and the others very small.

For the purposes of professional reflective practice, consideration of Johari window can be beneficial when dealing with both individuals and groups. It is a useful model to be used when considering your use of what are termed 'soft skills', which consist of active listening, empathy, co-operation, inter-group development and interpersonal development. Particularly useful to the new teachers is consideration of the unknown box, in which is contained your potential.

Think about the type of person you are. Do you like to keep things to yourself or are you a very open person? If you changed, what difference would that make to your relationship with others? What would you like to happen? What would you not like to happen?

Batari's box

Another model that is pertinent when dealing with people is that of Batari's box.

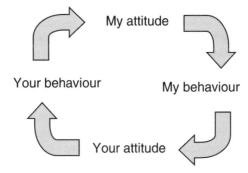

This model indicates the way in which two people can upset each other within seconds without actually meaning to do so. If you are in a bad mood or you are cross about something, the chances are that it is going to affect your attitude; probably unconsciously. This is fine for as long as you are alone, but when you interact with someone problems can occur. This model suggests that your attitude affects your behaviour, which affects their attitude, which affects their behaviour; this is simple, yet pertinent. When you meet another person, if you are carrying negative thoughts it is possible that they will show through, in which case your attitude is at that time negative and as a consequence this will have a direct bearing upon your behaviour.

Imagine the following scenario. You, a teacher, are walking along the corridor when you are greeted by an enthusiastic student. You are late because the traffic was awful and you must prepare for a very important meeting in less than five minutes; without interruption you may just make it. Now this student's presence is not helpful, you feel inclined not to stop walking as you engage in conversation and give scant attention to this person. They present you a wad of papers and ask you if you can have a quick look at their assignment. Now you are not happy as you know there is no such thing as a quick look at any assignment and in any case this is the third time they have bothered you. At the moment, the student is unaware of your difficulties getting to work, they had no idea that you are late for a meeting and they are further unaware that they are the fifth person to ask you to look at their work since yesterday morning. Had they done, they may have thought twice about the request.

From this point, it does not go well, your attitude towards this person is negative, and you are experiencing feelings of stress, annoyance and mild loathing. You arrive at outside your office door turn and say, *Look, I have seen your work, if you have done all I suggested in the feedback, then it is fine I am sure.* Here your attitude has affected your behaviour, which has now most certainly affected your student's attitude negatively. As an immediate response the student turns and walks away; you feel sure you hear some inappropriate language, but you tell yourself, it is too late now, the damage has been done and in any case the student is being totally self-centred.

Later, when you have calmed down, you begin to have second thoughts about the way in which you dealt with the student and begin to regret what happened. In fact, it bothers you so much you decide to use to situation for an example of your professional reflective practice. You record the situation as you remembered it and then reflect upon it. It is during the reflection that you ask yourself what the outcome would have been if you were not so annoyed at the time.

Emotions if not checked can reap havoc in seconds. The trick is to be aware of your state of mind and make a conscious effort to intervene. If you recognise that your attitude is negative, then intervention at the very first stage of Batari's box can save the day. If attitude affects behaviour then an awareness of this factor is the first step to modifying behaviour. The person walking along the corridor was presented fewer options in their emotional state. That is the problem with emotion, it is incredibly selfish and so there is normally only one preferred option – me.

If the person in the corridor had managed to break away from the emotional state, then arguably they would have been presented more options.

TASK TASK **TASK** TASK **TASK** TASK **TASK** TASK **TASK** TASK **TASK** TASK **TASK** TASK

Before reading on, think about what these options could have included?

These could have included:

- explaining to the student that you have no time right now, but if they can return at a specified time you can go over it with them one to one;
- being two minutes late for the meeting;
- having a general rule that the students can submit their work only once for feedback prior to marking;
- accepting work only via email so you can read it at a time that suits you.

The issues the person had may not be at first obvious to the casual observer. At first glance it appeared that the teacher was short of time; however, further consideration may indicate that the actual situation was that of poor time management aggravated by poor people and organisational skills; here the short-tempered teacher's behaviour was symptomatic of other problems.

An awareness of Batari's box enables you to first check your state of mind and then to consider if your present course is the most appropriate one. If it is not, you can change what you are doing before any harm is done. Obviously the model can be used in a more positive way where what you do is appreciated by the other party, but for the purpose of professional reflective practice, this will rarely cause concern or the need for further thought.

Think about a time or some times when your communication has gone terribly wrong with another person very quickly. What did you do? What could you have done differently?

Empty chair technique

The empty chair technique is a framework used to assist a person to consider the situation from a point of view other than their own. However, sometimes people do not know exactly what their point of view is, or they recognise that if their own point of view would infringe on the rights of another, they would change that point of view. Here there are three points of view, although there could be more if necessary. These are firstly the point of view of the teacher; next is that of the learner; and finally, that of an observer. When doing this it helps to use three different chairs.

As you are the teacher, it is useful for you to assume the first position in the teacher's chair. Whatever the situation is does not matter, what matters is that you are thinking about it. For this example we will consider that there is an issue that needs to be spoken about with a student and you are feeling troubled by it; maybe you just don't know where to start. You are now going to talk through the situation (in your head) as if the student were in front of you responding to what you are saying. Consider what you believe the situation is. Think about what you can see, what is being said and done, consider the emotional level. Think about the response that you are getting. Think about how it makes you feel.

Next, change seats; you are now in the student's seat. Imagine that you are the student and that you are hearing what the teacher is saying, experience your own words. Listen to what is being said and consider how you feel. How are you reacting? Why is this? What is your response?

Change seats again and now assume the position of the observer. Replay the situation again, and this time watch as the teacher explains the situation. Consider the reaction of the student. What can you see? What is happening? Does anything need to be changed, altered, or tempered? How is the teacher coming across and how is the student reacting. What have you learned about this encounter?

The limitations of this exercise are obvious: you are reacting as you alone would react and not the student. But the advantage of the empty chair technique is that people do not always consider how they are coming across, how they are being perceived. Sometimes they go blindly into a situation without considering how they will be received. This exercise enables you to experience what it is like to deal with yourself and then watch the situation as you interact with another.

Think about a situation that you may deal with in the near future. This can be any interaction. Go through the technique. What did you experience? What have you learned? What are you actually like to listen to and be with?

Thinking about organisational performance

SWOT analysis

Another useful technique is that of SWOT analysis. This is particularly constructive when attempting to identify where you are situated at a particular time and it can also be used as a strategic planning technique. SWOT stands for Strengths, Weaknesses, Opportunities and Threats. It can be broken down into two basic areas: the internal influences which are the 'strengths' and 'weaknesses' internal to the subject, and the external influences which are the 'opportunities' and 'threats' offered by the external environment.

In its simplest form it seeks to answer the following:

- How can I make best use of my strengths?
- How can I guard against my weaknesses?
- How can I seize the opportunities?
- How can I avoid the threats?

To contextualise this we will consider this SWOT analysis in terms of you applying for a new position. The job application form is asking you to state your qualities and so in order to achieve this it is advantageous to consider and answer the following.

Strengths

- What do I do well?
- What have been my most notable achievements?
- What are the reasons for my success?
- What knowledge or expertise will I bring to the organisation?
- What is my greatest asset?
- What are my motivating factors for applying for this job?
- How do I measure my success?

Weaknesses

- What could be improved about me?
- What do I do generally badly?
- What tasks should I avoid?
- What are my professional weaknesses?
- How do they affect my performance?
- What am I least able to do?

Opportunities

- What opportunities do I face?
- What is my particular area of expertise?
- Am I doing everything I can to enhance my opportunities?
- What formal training and education are necessary to open more doors?
- Would a further qualification be useful?

Threats

- What obstacles do I face?
- Does changing technology threaten me?

- Could my specific area of interest be diminishing in comparison with more developing fields?
- What factors might negatively affect my future employment?
- Will my forthcoming job provide access to new challenges to keep me up to date in the event of redundancy?

The above is one example for which SWOT analysis is useful. The benefit of this analysis is that it can assist the user to obtain an accurate, all-round description of the particular circumstances at a point in time. As a result decisions can be made from an informed basis. It can be a useful tool at a fork in your career where you are unsure of which route to take. SWOT analysis will enable you to make an informed decision based on fact.

Performance needs analysis

As the name suggests, performance needs analysis (PNA) is a tool that can be used to identify what is lacking in relation to a person's or an organisation's performance. Essentially it is a form of gap analysis. The technique is very simple, but effective, and comprises of three questions.

The first question is, *What is required?* Normally this question will result because of a change of policy or legislation; often both. The nature of your role changes continuously, sometimes hugely, more often in small yet significant steps. When a change occurs it is necessary for you to identify what exactly you are being asked to do. In this instance we will assume that you have been asked to record your students' progress more accurately. A report is expected following each taught session and it must identify the progress made during the session and list the content of the agreed action plans, which must be signed, dated and SMART.

Now you have identified what is required, the next step is to ask the next question, *What are you actually doing now?* Here you identify your practices, habits, procedures, standard operating procedures, relevant memos, policies, best practices and whatever else you can lay your hands on. From these you identify what you are actually doing. (Let us assume for the sake of argument that practice and policy are congruent.)

The last question is this, *Comparing the first and second questions, what are the perceived gaps?* An honest interpretation of the data can reap rewards. Often it is assumed by those who assume to know, that the answer is obvious. However, it is not until the questions have been considered comprehensively that factors which may not have been previously considered may become significant influencing factors.

Conclusion

This chapter has offered a number of models and techniques considered suitable to assist your professional reflective practice. However, these models and techniques are not intended to sit alone, perhaps used once and then discarded. They are offered to you in support of your CPD. They will take practice and not all will be appropriate for every situation. The content of this chapter is not an exhaustive list by any means, but if you are interested in the topics discussed it is hoped that you may find the references and further reading useful.

A SUMMARY OF **KEY POINTS**

In this chapter we have looked at the following key points.

> **A description of the term 'psycholateral approach' in relation to professional reflective practice.**

> **Consideration of the three domains within education and learning in relation to your own progress and developmental issues.**

> **An explanation of the terms 'thinking about thinking', 'thinking about relationships' and 'thinking about organisational performance'.**

> **An explanation of the terms, personal filters, levels of awareness and levels of competence in relation to your own thinking.**

> **Techniques to support your relationships with others, such as, Johari window, Batari's box and the empty chair technique.**

> **Consideration of SWOT and performance needs analysis to support your understanding of your organisational performance.**

> **Relating your reflections to your professional practice by applying the techniques and models described within this chapter.**

REFERENCES AND FURTHER READING REFERENCES AND FURTHER READING

Bavister, S and Vickers, A (2004) *Teach yourself NLP*. London: Hodder.

Bradbury, A (2006) *Develop your NLP skills* (3rd edition). London: Kogan Page.

Churches R and Terry R (2007) *NLP for teachers: how to be a highly effective teacher*. Carmarthen: Crown House.

Knight, S (2002) *NLP at work. Neuro linguistic programming. The difference that makes a difference in business*. London: Nicholas Brearly.

Luft, J (1969) *Of human interaction*. Mountain View, CA: Mayfield Publishing Company.

McDermott, I and Jago, W (2001) *The NLP coach: a comprehensive guide to personal well-being and professional success*. London: Piatkus.

McDermot, I and Shircore, I (1999) *Manage yourself, manage your life: Simple NLP techniques for success and happiness*. London: Piatkus.

Pease, A and Pease, B (2004) *The definitive book of body language: how to read others' attitudes by their gestures*. London: Orion.

5
Types of continuing professional development

By the end of this chapter you will be able to:

- **list a range of activities that may be appropriate for CPD;**
- **distinguish between activities that cover CPD in your subject specialism and those with a focus on teaching and learning;**
- **reflect on how activities already undertaken have contributed to your CPD.**

Professional Standards

This chapter relates to the following Professional Standards.

Professional Values:

AS 4 Reflection and evaluation of their own practice and their continuing professional development as teachers.

Professional Knowledge and Understanding:

AK 4.3 Ways to reflect, evaluate and use research to develop own practice, and to share good practice with others.

Professional Practice:

AP 4.2 Reflect on and demonstrate commitment to improvement of own personal and teaching skills through regular evaluation and use of feedback.

AP 4.3 Share good practice with others and engage in continuing professional development through reflection, evaluation and the appropriate use of research.

Introduction

This chapter examines the various activities that can be undertaken as part of your CPD. The IfL (2008) observes that *CPD is most effective when practitioners reflect on their professional practice, develop a personal plan based on their identified needs and match this against their organisational context and development plan.* There are three distinct elements referred to here. First is the reflection in relation to your own professional practice. Second is the development of a personal plan, based on identified needs. Your personal plan and identified needs can be linked to your appraisal and are normally expressed in terms of SMART objectives. Third is the matching of these against the organisational context and development plan. Your appraisal will align itself towards the needs of your organisation and its future development.

You may wonder what activities will be suitable for your own CPD. The IfL (2008) suggests that all forms of professional development, accredited and non-accredited, will be valued and recognised. It is further suggested that your CPD should not be limited to attendance on structured courses; instead it advocates a range of professional development activities. When considering the suitability of any activity ask yourself the following.

- Does this activity link to my professional practice?
- Does this relate to my personal plan (appraisal)?
- Does this match against the organisational context and development plan?
- Will this impact upon my learners?

If all four questions are answered positively then you can assume that the activity is suitable. However, not all activities will be directly linked to your personal plan and it is recognised that the organisational content may be tangential. What is most important is that you can identify how the activity links to your professional practice and how it is likely to impact upon your learners. Remember, in Chapter 2 the term 'dual professionalism' was explained as a characteristic of the lifelong learning sector: you need to be a professional in your own subject specialism as well as in teaching and learning. The implication of this is that the CPD you undertake can be relevant to your subject specialism, for instance keeping up with the latest developments in motor vehicle engineering or travel and tourism. Alternatively, your CPD activities can be relevant to teaching and learning, for instance developing new resources to teach your subject, trying out different teaching strategies or methods after reading up on a learning theory, or looking at ways to differentiate your teaching to meet the needs of your learners. For your 30 hours of CPD, or the required pro-rata hours, you can mix and match between the two types of CPD. Ideally you're looking for a range of activities covering your subject specialism and teaching and learning.

TASK TASK **TASK** TASK **TASK TASK** TASK **TASK** TASK **TASK TASK** TASK

List the CPD activities you have been involved in over the last year, dividing them into 'subject specialism' and 'teaching and learning'.

How do you know how much time each activity is 'worth' towards your total hours of CPD? To offer guidance, some awarding bodies have designed a 'tariff'. The tariff indicates how many hours you can claim for completion of a CPD activity. You may be awarded a certificate of attendance for a certain number of hours, which you can use as supporting evidence. However, the tariff is for recognised programmes and courses only. Although some of your CPD will be of this nature, many more activities will be less formal. As an autonomous professional you make your own decisions as to how much time you claim for the activities you undertake. This may result in different teachers claiming different amounts of time for the same activity. There is no right or wrong. CPD is highly individual; only you know how much time you have spent on a certain activity. You may claim half an hour for reading an article in a journal and reflecting on the impact on your learners, whereas your colleague may claim an hour for reading the same article. Perhaps your colleague reads at a slightly slower pace or takes longer to reflect on the impact. Perhaps you were already familiar with the concepts discussed in the article but they were new to your colleague. The important issue is your professional development and how your learners will benefit from this development. Although the allocation of hours, and what is acceptable to the IfL, may seem a bit vague and some might suggest open to abuse by claiming more hours than spent, ultimately the decision is yours. Your integrity is at stake, it's not a competition in who gets away with doing the least (by claiming the most). After all, you need and want to stay on top of the latest developments in your field, and, as a professional teacher, are interested in how to improve or fine-tune your practice. Some of the activities you undertake could easily 'fill' your required hours in one claim. For instance, you're doing your PTLLS, CTLLS, DTLLS, Cert Ed, PGCE or a BA, BSc or MA in your subject specialism. Each of those covers more than 30 hours. However, you need to show evidence of undertaking a range of activities, so you will still have to participate in other CPD events and reflect on their impact.

What activities can count towards your total hours of CPD? To assist you in deciding what to consider, the following activities are discussed in more detail and some examples of how to use them are given. The list is not exhaustive and the activities are not in a hierarchical order. Some may link together: a change in your role can mean having to deliver, or get involved in, a new course or programme, for which you may need to gain a new formal qualification. The examples are adapted, real-life accounts of how teachers have engaged in CPD activities; they are not entries to reflective portfolios. Their purpose is to help you recognise situations that can count towards your CPD requirements. We would like to thank all for their ideas and contributions.

- Obtaining a formal qualification
- Training courses and workshops
- Attending a conference or seminar
- Delivering or developing a new course
- Attending meetings
- Research projects
- Reading an article or book
- Peer observation
- A change in your role
- Improving your teaching
- Secondment

Activities suitable for continuing professional development

Obtaining a formal qualification

Formal qualifications can be either in your own subject specialism, such as a BA, BSc, MA, PhD or a formal vocational qualification, or with a focus on teaching and learning, such as initial teacher training programmes (PTLLS, CTLLS, DTLLS, Cert Ed, PGCE, etc). Each of those courses requires much more of the time than you need as evidence to maintain your professional standing and IfL membership. However, as you need a range of CPD activities, we recommend, as a guideline, that you allocate half of your total hours of CPD to obtaining a formal qualification. Some of the formal qualifications incorporate a reflective element, such as keeping a diary or a reflective module. In this case, you're meeting a large part of your CPD requirements while obtaining your qualification. Trainee teachers on a teacher training programme may find this reassuring as the programme counts towards their CPD. The following is an example of undertaking a vocational qualification.

> *I am a State Registered Paramedic. As specialist vocational instructors we are used to teaching a subject that we are experienced in. However, there are areas of Ambulance Aid that although important are not regularly encountered. The lack of personal experience in these subjects leads to our reluctance to teach these sessions. Child abuse is one such subject. We usually ask external specialists to take the session, as they have better and more in-depth knowledge. However, they often have a limited understanding of Ambulance Aid. Therefore, my aim was to*

undertake an external course of sufficient depth, run by the NSPCC, that will not just improve my clinical practice, but also allows me to provide an informed, and relevant, session to my students.

This course has not only improved my care as an operational paramedic, but has allowed me to provide a more informed training session.

I taught the child abuse session on one of our basic training courses. There are a wide range of physical and behavioural signs that are potential indicators of one of four types of abuse. This is where the information from my course became really useful. Later, I broke the group into syndicates to review some imaginary scenarios. I asked each syndicate to identify what, if any, type of abuse was taking place and what actions they would take. I then asked them to present their scenario and thoughts to the group as a whole. My aim was to make them consider child abuse, but to accept that a definitive judgement of whether abuse is taking place falls out of our purview. We can, and should, only be open to the possibility, and carefully record all potential indicators. It highlights that it is important that we are not judgemental and where possible remain emotionally detached. If we believe that an immediate threat exists, we refer this to the police.

My post-session reflection identified that I needed more time for the session in order to deliver it in a more student centred fashion. There is a lot of information that I wanted to pass to the students. Due to the time constraints, I gave a lot of this information in a traditional 'talk and chalk' PowerPoint presentation. The lesson would have been improved with a greater degree of student involvement. Considerations for future sessions include some form of guided discovery learning of the signs of abuse, as well as more scenario-based activities, perhaps including carefully selected photographs of child abuse victims.

The students advised that they found the session very 'scary', 'interesting' and 'thought-provoking'. Many advised that they found the case study and scenarios very helpful and would have enjoyed more of these. Some advised that they found the PowerPoint interesting but less enjoyable. None identified any areas that they did not regard as relevant. Some advised that they might contact the NSPCC with regard to undertaking the same course themselves in due course. I achieved my objectives with this project. Through reflection on the lesson I have identified room for improvement. It will be better next time.

Training courses and workshops

Training courses and workshops are perhaps the most obvious means of ensuring CPD. We refer here to the in-house style of training offered to staff by their employers. This can be provided either by members from within the organisation who benefit from specific knowledge or can be delivered by outside organisations. When considering the suitability of this for CPD, it is highly likely that there will be a direct link between the activity and your professional practice. Often the training will be delivered because of an identified need as a result of the appraisals that have taken place. It could be for instance that a number of teachers have identified that they need (more) training on how to effectively use an interactive whiteboard in their teaching. Organisations will respond by arranging appropriate training for those members of staff. Alternatively, the need may have been identified in an Ofsted inspection or a performance issue. Performance needs analysis (PNA) can also be used to identify failings in relation to an organisation's performance, the results of which will inform subsequent performance issues. One option available to an organisation to improve organisational performance is training. An example of this is given below.

I am a teacher in supported learning department at an FE college. I recently attended a workshop on interactive voting systems. Each student has their own 'voting button' and is able to affect and change the data on-screen by placing their vote. The voting system at my own organisation is not the 'Millionaire' system but one made by the whiteboard supplier we already use. This was useful to me, as I was already familiar with the icons and their positions on screen. I found myself quite nervous of using this technology as none of my other colleagues had used it and therefore could offer no advice on its use, but I should not have worried as it is very user-friendly. The makers have an internet forum where teachers who have used their system have posted video clips with advice. The company also have interactive demonstration on their website to show some of the ways the system can be used and I would like to try some of these in the future, particularly for sign language as I think this resource has a great many possibilities in this field. I adapted a 'Who wants to be a millionaire' presentation, as it was fun and I felt my students would like the familiar format. Although it is possible to input the names of each individual, so that the class can see exactly who was right and wrong, for my first lesson using the system I decided not to do this as I felt it might affect the confidence of some of my students. I now feel that I was being over-anxious as my class actually told each other when they had made wrong choices, and in future I will include this feature as I think it will not only enhance the enjoyment of the exercise but will aid me in my record-keeping.

As a learning tool I think these systems have a number of advantages. The whole class participates and concentrates fully on the task, the feedback they receive is instant, which reinforces learning, as does the competitive element of the system. Less able students have the questions read out. Students with conditions such as ADHD or ADD who, when given a normal questionnaire, race ahead without thinking fully are forced to pace themselves as they cannot answer a question until an icon on-screen has been touched and, conversely, students with autism must make a decision and move on, as the screen shows who has yet to vote. For the teacher there are the advantages of being in control, of having evidence of a discussion-type lesson and it is possible to keep records of results which can be referred to later to assess learning and track individuals.

I feel my class enjoyed using this resource immensely and I will definitely use it again in future when possible, as I think it has huge potential for students in my department and can do much to alleviate their problems.

Overall I feel I have gained a great deal from this exercise. Having initially been very wary of any form of technology, I would now happily use such multimedia tools as PowerPoint, video, an interactive whiteboard and interactive voting systems in my classroom.

I have not finished with my study of technology yet; I think my next area of exploration will be desktop virtual reality as this may be a way of overcoming the problems of access to visit sites and transport. Although I would never recommend it as a replacement for such visits, it may be a useful tool.

Attending meetings

It may not be immediately obvious how a meeting could be considered suitable for CPD. Essentially there are two types of meetings: those held to provide information and those where decisions are made. For example, a member of the team has been to a conference held by an awarding body such as City and Guilds, Edexcel, OCR, etc., and wishes to share the information with other members of the team. It may be that the latest developments required by the awarding body have an impact on your practice and therefore your students. You will need to reflect on how you can modify your practice based on the information cascaded from the colleague who attended the conference. Remember, meetings suitable for CPD can be either formal or informal in nature; their suitability is a matter for you. For example, an entry for a CPD portfolio could look as follows.

Last Friday I attended a staff meeting where we discussed our external verifier's report. The EV pointed out in her report that our candidates produce too much evidence, resulting in vast portfolios. She suggested that the candidates take a more holistic approach, making use of cross-referencing. This way, they can use a piece of writing or a witness statement to meet more than one performance indicator. Further to that, more evidence can be gathered by the assessors by carrying out observations. The impact on me is that I have to arrange more observations in the workplace with my candidates. This is not always easy, as the observations have to fit in with the employers. It also means more time for travel. However, the marking of completed units will be less time-consuming. This will benefit the assessors and the verification process. The next cohort will start in September and I will explain to the candidates the importance of arranging observations to tick off performance indicators. Perhaps this will help in making the portfolios a less daunting task for the students.

Research projects

A research project is an activity that enables you to find out something about a topic or subject to improve your practice. The topic of your research can either be subject specific, which means finding out something about your subject specialism, or it can be an investigation in how to improve your teaching and students' learning. Research projects can be a small and informal activity or can be part of your academic studies. Some teacher training programmes include modules on professional development. Time spent on completing these modules can form part of your total hours required for CPD.

A small piece of action research could serve to identify whether a particular teaching strategy is appropriate. On the other hand, your research project could aim to identify how to meet the learning needs of some of your students. This may involve reading around the subject, talking to your students and contacting relevant organisations or associations that specialise in that subject. This may result in a formal report which can be shared with colleagues in a team meeting or even other institutions. The following is an example of such a research project.

I work with adults with learning difficulties and some of them have autism. I know very little about autism and have decided to research this topic in order to increase my awareness of this condition. There are various degrees of autism and I am looking to increase my knowledge of this subject so that I can help learners to reach their full potential in the classroom. I will investigate different methods, resources and activities to aid my teaching by reading relevant literature, websites and by contacting the National Autistic Society.

My research suggests that providing one-to-one contact, where possible, is an effective method for teaching the autistic learner. They respond well to this kind of support and benefit from the extra attention. Furthermore, to meet the needs of learners on the lower end of the autistic spectrum, I will use a symbol-based computer program to create worksheets. According to my research, this is a very effective resource, as the learner can recognise symbols and point to each picture in response to a question. Using the trace font when creating worksheets also enables the learner to copy over familiar words, such as their name. This process will eventually lead to the learner forming the letters themselves and then writing their name independently.

By identifying learners' needs, their strengths, weaknesses, communication and social difficulties and sharing this information with any other tutors and learning support staff, we will all be better prepared to assist and support the learner in class.

Reading an article or book

Probably all teachers read articles in journals or books (or websites) to keep up to date with the latest developments or just to look something up. Sometimes, the article may have an impact on your practice. This can be either from a subject-specific perspective (you have learnt something new about your subject that you want to share with your learners) or from a teaching and learning perspective (after reading about experiential learning you would like to give this a try in class). The reading can contribute to and form part of your CPD, although it is probably not pre-planned. All you need to do is reflect on the book or article, and on the impact the reading has had on your learners. Make sure all your reading is properly referenced. Books and articles in journals benefit from being reviewed and refereed before publication; articles on websites are not and may lack rigour. Consider the following example.

Recently I have been thinking about my relationship with the students in my class and in particular the way in which I communicate with them. Some of the more immature students are behaving like children. Their attitude seems to be that I am responsible for their learning. Although they attend the lessons, there seems to be a 'them and us' mentality. I feel I am missing something, but I don't know what it is exactly. What I do know is that the students will get on a lot better if they would just do something for themselves. My colleague calls them the PlayStation generation because she says that they get everything they want there and then and have never actually had to think for themselves.

I was discussing this with my colleague and she suggested that I dip into Reece and Walker's book Teaching, training and learning, *because there is a chapter on communication and the teacher. The chapter was good and what I found to be most relevant to me was the part on transactional analysis. I hadn't realised there are different ego states. I had never heard of the parent, child and adult ego states and how, if you are in one particular ego state, you almost invite a reaction from another ego state. I suppose, when I'm in class, I take on the critical parent ego state, thereby inviting a child ego state response. No wonder my students behave like needy, demanding children, stamping their feet.*

This has changed now, not just what I do but how I think about things. Now I feel that I understand what is happening under the surface. I hadn't realised how much of a difference the use of language can make to communication. I don't just mean the words I choose but more from where I am coming from. I can see now that if the ego state is not appropriate, I can go some way to changing it so that I can communicate on the adult-to-adult level. I will not let the students wind me up, so that I become a critical parent to their child ego state, but keep to the adult–adult state. The students have responded well to my change in behaviour and communication patterns, making my lessons more enjoyable for all.

Peer observation

In teaching, you generally learn best from trying out things for yourself. However, you can also learn from observing the teaching of your colleagues or peers. Depending on the focus, this can be in the same subject specialism that you teach or in a different one. Perhaps you would like to see how one of the other members of your team or department teaches a certain topic. The topic might be new to you or you may be looking at different ways of delivering the topic. Alternatively, you may want to observe a colleague who teaches a different subject, to get some fresh ideas. Although the subject is different, the teacher may be employing teaching strategies or methods of assessment that can be modified for your own teaching. How do they differentiate to meet the needs of individual learners; is the pace of the lesson appropriate; how are core skills (or skills for life) embedded? You may want to focus on classroom management. If you find a particular group of learners challenging and you hear in the staffroom that one of your colleagues does not have the same problems, it may be useful to observe for yourself how your colleague manages the classroom and interacts with the learners. Consider the following example.

I am an ESOL tutor, teaching two evening classes a week. The lesson I observed for one hour was not in my own subject area but an AS level psychology class. There were 24 students in the class, sitting in six groups of four. The teacher started the session with a recap from last week and introduced today's topic. Next, she gave each group a piece of research to analyse and discuss. The subjects were displayed on the interactive whiteboard. After 10 minutes, two students from each group had to move to another group and explain the research they had analysed to the others. The teacher had given me a lesson plan at the start of the lesson; she referred to this activity as 'jig-sawing'. She kept repeating the exercise until all students had covered all pieces of research. The activity worked very well. All students moved around and had to explain their findings to the others, they were all engaged and there was a real buzz in the class with high energy levels. My lessons can be quiet at times and students stay where they are, usually in the same seat every lesson. Although I encourage interaction between the students, as it is a good opportunity for them to practise their English skills, they only talk to their 'friend' next to them. To boost energy levels and ensure interaction I will try the jig-saw exercise. I can differentiate the tasks by giving groups an article to read and analyse, according to their ability. I am pleased I observed the psychology class, as I would not have considered a jig-saw activity before. As far as I'm aware none of my colleagues use this teaching strategy; perhaps, if it goes well, they can observe my class!

Attending a conference or seminar

Conferences or seminars can be very informative. There may be more than one speaker and different topics may be covered. Conferences can be in your own subject specialism, as it is important to keep informed of the latest developments in industry, or in teaching and learning. As there may be costs attached to attending a conference (fee and travel expenses for instance), you may be the only one from your team attending. You may therefore be tasked with taking notes and collecting all material available (handouts, leaflets, information packs or delegate packs) which you are asked to share with your colleagues in a team meeting, 'cascading down' the information. Having to tell others what you have learned means you really have to focus on the information given and consider the relevance to your practice. Below is an example.

> *I recently attended a seminar on 'Behaviour Management: Dealing with Difficult Students'. We all have difficult students in our classes, students who don't seem to want to be there, disrupting the learning for others. I really wanted to find out how to deal more effectively with these students, to learn some strategies. I will be the only one from our department who is attending, as no one else could be released. The speaker got us to explain what we mean by the term 'difficult behaviour'. It really got down to our own expectations of our students. Next we looked at causes for the difficult behaviour, putting everything into context. After that, proactive and reactive techniques to deal with difficult behaviour were discussed, with a focus on minimising potential problems. I will try these techniques with my students next week. There's one student in particular who always challenges everything I say, always talks back, has a negative attitude and is disrespectful to his peers. Rather than getting annoyed and angry with him, I will try to find out what causes his behaviour and perhaps find a solution. I will also do some further reading, as the speaker gave us some useful publications. I will share the information with my colleagues in the next team meeting, give them copies of the PowerPoint presentation and discuss my notes. The seminar was very useful, I hope the strategies will work.*

Delivering or developing a new course

There may be a time in your teaching career when you're asked to deliver or develop a new course. This can be time-consuming but is also very exciting. You will need to read up about the subject, check the accreditation, if appropriate, and ensure the level is correct. You need to know the assessment criteria and decide on the most appropriate assessment methods. How will you deliver the new programme and what resources are available? It may seem a daunting task but one that can give a huge amount of job satisfaction, as in the following example.

> *I work for the prison service, in a young offender's institution, and have been asked to deliver a new course on Understanding Eating Disorders. I spent two weeks gaining information. I contacted The Eating Disorders Association (www.edauk.-com). They were very helpful and directed me to several websites. In addition I contacted beat (www.b-eat.co.uk). They sent me a short course called 'Body Talk – building body confidence'. This looks at self-esteem and body language. I will look at this as a supplementary resource as this would probably best be delivered as a separate course.*

I directed the majority of my research to the internet. I downloaded a massive amount of literature. I realised that there was so much more to eating disorders than I had originally thought. The problem is that I would be in danger of exceeding the expectations of a level 1 outcome by including too much information. A level 1 course does not require analysis or further information, only facts, such as; students will employ a narrow range of applied knowledge, basic comprehension, demonstrate a narrow range of skills, present and record information from readily available sources. I downloaded several pictures from the internet that I felt would be both shocking and informative when put into the right context. These would form the basis of some group discussion. Further I had started to watch a programme on television on ITV called 'Supersize V Superskinny', which was just what was needed as a visual resource. I recorded an episode onto DVD for later use.

Before starting to write the course I approached the accreditations controller for the prison. I asked her for any guidelines that she knew of that would enable me to write the course to the standard required by the National Open College Network (NOCN). I gained valuable assistance from her, as she was aware of the current specifications.

I decided to pilot the course with a group of six students, of mixed abilities and ethnic backgrounds, all aged between 18 and 21 years old. Over the next two days I delivered the course. The subject caused a great forum for discussion, with all students really getting excited and wanting their own input. All resources were well received, particularly the tasting of different foods. The students completed all written exercises to an appropriate standard for the level of the course. I felt that this was a great success. Prior to starting this project I would not have believed I could develop a course and so now feel enthusiastic about further challenges in this domain. The feedback from the students was very positive and of great encouragement to me.

I had a visit from the external moderator from NOCN just after delivering the pilot. She has given her approval for the course to be delivered on a wider scale. My development on a personal level has been that I feel I am more than a teacher, as I am now able to extend the provision of the curriculum within the catering and hospitality department, and extended the social knowledge of this group of individuals. I have extended and developed my computer skills and used these to produce more engaging and informative resources. This will help to develop the education of my students and hopefully encourage them to gain employment on release and avoid re-offending. Prior to developing this course I had been guilty of perhaps doing too much of the talking in the classroom, but with this course I decided to encourage more student-led discussion. This has changed my classroom manner and made me look at existing courses with a view to change. I will address these in the near future.

A change in your role

A change in role often requires more professional development. A change can be a move sideways, which means you're teaching similar subjects as before but perhaps through a different awarding body, requiring you to get to know the new programme and assessment criteria, or it can be an extension of your current role. The change can be a move upwards through promotion. Perhaps you are now responsible for the internal verification process of a course you have so far been an assessor on. You need to familiarise yourself with the process and procedures and gain a V1 Award. Alternatively, the change is a complete one, you're leaving your current role to start something fresh. An example of this is changing from teaching your subject specialism to becoming involved in teacher training. In any of these scenarios more CPD is required. The following is an example of a role that has been extended.

Until now my specialist subject has been food safety. Working within the health and safety department in the Prison Service my role extends beyond food safety and will now involve teaching a range of subjects falling under health and safety. I intend to undertake some formal training to ensure my knowledge is at a sufficiently high level and current. Keeping up to date with your specialist subject is vital to be able to speak with authority and confidence, comfortable that your information is reliable and current. As well as reading on the subject of health and safety, I will attend suitable conferences and exhibitions to ensure I continually develop within my specialist area.

The subject of health and safety gets a very poor press, it's often considered boring by learners invited on to a course and yet it touches everyone at work. All my skills, knowledge and enthusiasm will be needed to deliver a course that brings the subject to life, leaves the learners aware and motivated.

At the beginning of the year arrangements were made to allow me to sit in on at least two Health and Safety Awareness courses. Observing these sessions allowed me to note everything from the room layout, resources used, format of the presentation, arrangements for differentiation and types of formative and summative assessments used. The course is prescribed by the Prison Service and is in the form of a PowerPoint presentation. At this stage my own lesson plan started to take shape. My learners won't be sitting listening all the time, group work will get them on their feet and allow them to voice their opinions, put forward ideas and feed back to the wider group.

As part of my progression to presenting the full course, my next step was to present a one-hour session. Despite all the preparation and increased knowledge of the subject my concentration was on the PowerPoint slides, links from slide to slide were shaky or non-existent, my awareness of the group of students was poor; I was not catering for their needs. Reviewing my performance and getting feedback from the health and safety awareness tutor was very beneficial and leaves me full of confidence to be able to fulfil my extended role within our health and safety department.

My journey has taken about four months. It has been a very productive time, having increased my knowledge of health and safety to a level at which my teaching can now cover a wider range of topics.

Improving your teaching

Improving your teaching, or enhancing your learners' experience is at the centre of all CPD. You want to develop your skills, knowledge, etc., to become a better teacher. This should always be your main focus. As your teaching improves, your learners benefit, enhancing their experience, which impacts on learner retention and achievement figures. In the current climate there is an increasing emphasis on success rates, affecting college funding, hence the importance of retention and achievement.

How can you improve your teaching? Knowing your learners is at the heart of this. You can then decide which teaching strategies would work best. Perhaps you can improve your resources or differentiate more to meet individual learners' needs. The following is an example of improving teaching by using different resources.

I am a maths teacher. My aim is to design suitable resources for teaching calculus to vocational learners.

One of my main areas for professional development over the past few years has been to incorporate more ICT into my lessons as this is a resource I have not been very confident with. Now I have had time to review what is available on the web and given some thought as to how and when I can incorporate it, I will be able to improve my teaching in this area. Four of the six websites I looked at had very good applets to demonstrate the basic concept of differentiation: that is, how the gradient curve changes continuously, and at the same time graph out the derivative. Similar good applets for integration are available showing how it is used to find areas and volumes of complicated shapes.

The first resources I actually incorporated into my lessons were some PowerPoint presentations I used with my HND learners. The integration resources were particularly good for vocational learners as they use velocity, time, distance travelled and acceleration in the examples. The response from the learners was positive but there was an initial groan at 'yet another PowerPoint presentation'. The fact that the subject matter had been put into context was the main plus point here. The usual questions of when and how will this new topic in maths ever be useful to them as engineers did not arise as the practical aspect was evident from the outset. This was the kind of response I was hoping for and there was a clear benefit for the learners and for me to have successfully used a new teaching method.

Secondment

On some occasion it may be useful for you to spend some time at a different institution or establishment to widen your experience. It may be that you return to industry for a short period of time to update your skills; or perhaps the other institution is more experienced in delivering certain programmes. It could be that you're asked to look at how a college, recently awarded a grade 1 in their Ofsted inspection, operate with a view to share best practice. The following is an example of sharing best practice in a uniformed environment.

As a police officer I am responsible for the training of Family Liaison Officers. To meet diversity needs I want to investigate death rituals practised by various different cultures and races. In order to do this I spent some time with a neighbouring police force as they are more experienced in dealing with the needs of ethnic minority groups.

The role of Family Liaison Officer is one of the most difficult and exacting positions within the police. They can be called whenever there is a need for a Family Liaison Officer and will be on call day and night on a rotational basis. The information I gathered will be helpful to any Family Liaison Officer that is assigned to a non-

Christian family. The research I have conducted in relation to the various death rituals performed by other than Christian religions, and subsequent teaching of the subject, should help Family Liaison Officers in their role. If they are more educated and aware of different families' requirements then this can only improve the service they give to bereaved families. It cannot lessen the family's sadness at losing a loved one but it can hopefully prevent exacerbating a delicate episode in their lives.

I have acquired copies of Faces of Britain, *which is a publication put together by a Police Community Trust. The students are able to retain a copy of this publication for future reference. Further, my teaching incorporates group work where the students will get together to discuss the similarities and differences between the different races and religions. Next, there will be a plenary discussion where we will discuss how best they can deal with the different aspects of these religions; how they will assist the families and how they can attempt to minimise the confusion that these families may be experiencing. Unfortunately, until I get feedback from any of the Family Liaison Officers which have dealt with the different religious beliefs on their role, I will not be aware if this input has assisted. Every family will obviously deal with grief in their own way and it is not possible to generalise and assume that what works for one family will work with all families.*

The above are all genuine examples of activities that teachers have undertaken to show their commitment to CPD. Some are focused on developing subject-specific knowledge, others on improving teaching and learning. In all the scenarios, the CPD undertaken had a positive impact on teaching practice, enhancing the learners' experience. If you have engaged in any other activities which have been beneficial to your practice, please contact us with your examples on www.QTLS.net.

A SUMMARY OF **KEY POINTS**

In this chapter we have looked at the following key points.

> **A range of activities have been listed that may be appropriate for CPD.**

> **Due to the nature of dual professionalism in the sector you can distinguish between activities that cover CPD in your own subject specialism and those with a focus on teaching and learning.**

> **The given examples of engagement in CPD will help you to reflect on and plan for your own CPD.**

REFERENCES AND FURTHER READING

Cross, V, Caladine, L, Morris, J, Hilton, R, Bristow, H and Moore, A (2006) *The practice-based educator: a reflective tool for CPD and accreditation*. Chichester: John Wiley and Sons.

Hitching, J (2008) *Maintaining your licence to practice*. Exeter: Learning Matters.

Institute for Learning (2007) *Guidelines for your continuing professional development (CPD)*. Available as a pdf at www.ifl.ac.uk.

Institute for Learning (2008) *CPD information*. www.ifl.ac.uk, accessed 11 August 2008.

Koshi, V (2005) *Action research for improving practice: a practical guide*. London: Sage.

McNiff, J and Whitehead, J (2006) *All you need to know about action research*. London: Sage.

6
Strategies and structure of reflective writing

By the end of this chapter you will be able to:

- identify an appropriate structure for your reflective writing;
- recognise the key characteristics of three pro formas;
- explain the range and extent of your CPD portfolio entry;
- recognise the supporting role of information technology;
- demystify common information technology terminology;
- identify the activities available within Institute for Learning's Reflect software.

Professional Standards

This chapter relates to the following Professional Standards.

Professional Values:

AS 4 Reflection and evaluation of their own practice and their continuing professional development as teachers.

Professional Knowledge and Understanding:

AK 4.3 Ways to reflect, evaluate and use research to develop own practice, and to share good practice with others.

Professional Practice:

AP 4.2 Reflect on and demonstrate commitment to improvement of own personal and teaching skills through regular evaluation and use of feedback.

AP 4.3 Share good practice with others and engage in continuing professional development through reflection, evaluation and the appropriate use of research.

Introduction

This chapter examines the various strategies and structure of reflective practice available to you as you begin to record your CPD. It does this by offering three pro formas designed at various levels to assist you as you complete your CPD entry. The specific contents of a CPD entry are identified, building incrementally over the three pro formas. Consideration is then given to the use of information technology (IT), where the rise in the use of IT and the difficulties some experience with the technical terminology are discussed. A 'jargon buster' is offered to demystify common IT terminology (see Appendix). The Institute for Learning's Reflect software package is described, identifying its purpose and the various aspects and uses available to the user.

How to do it, where to start

There will come the time when you have made your decision regarding the topic of your CPD portfolio entry and you are ready to put fingers to keyboard. At this point you have two main choices: you can either make your entry directly into your own computer at home or at work if that is appropriate, or if you are a member of the Institute for Learning (IfL), you can take advantage of their internet site by using the Reflect Pebble Pad e-portfolio system. We recognise that there is a third option of writing in longhand but due to its inflexibility it is not recommended.

For many, actually making that initial start to your CPD portfolio can be the most difficult stage of any writing. Because of this we recommend that at first you don't think too much about how you are going to do it, just do it. That way you will have something on a page that you reshape and work with later. Some people find that the process of writing down an experience is useful as it presents them with the space and time to think about something. You may find that verbalising an experience is not the same as recording it in words, as the latter is a much slower process, freeing up the brain which is now able to think around the subject as you write. As a result, the written account may be far richer and insightful than just the spoken word.

Using your computer

When writing your portfolio entry, it will assist you to identify the general area in which your entry will inhabit. Chapter 3 referred to the SCOPE mnemonic under the following headings:

- Social;
- Communicational;
- Organisational;
- Personal;
- Economic.

Obviously you are not restricted to these headings alone, they are simply designed to assist you and clarify your thoughts. Below is a pro forma that is offered for your entries.

Professional Reflective Practice Account Pro forma 1 (PRP1)

Date..

Nature of experience: S, C, O, P, E, Other..

My experience	
My reaction	
My analysis	
My interpretation	
My action plan	
Time allocated to this task	**Total time**

This pro forma can be reproduced using the Table tool in a Word document or can be cut and pasted from our associated website at www.qtls.net. The idea of the pro forma is to structure your account under the various headings. It is intended to assist your thinking by offering suggested topics to write about. You will notice the pro forma begins with an account of the experience as this is the most likely starting point for any piece of reflective account. However, the amount of descriptive writing will vary as you become accustomed to writing reflectively. The pro forma guides you through suggested topics and ends with an action plan. Your next reflective account can then begin either with a new experience or the action plan; it is entirely your choice.

Experience

Within this model you begin your account by describing the experience. This has the benefit of drawing your attention to the facts or order of events: this is particularly useful if the event was some time ago. Put yourself back in the situation and try to relive the experience. Ask yourself, what can you see, hear, feel, etc?

Reaction

Your reaction to the experience may be written in terms of how you reacted physically, mentally or emotionally. The distinction between your physical, mental and emotional reaction is that of a hand, head and heart response, or in other words:

- hand – what you did physically;
- head – your logical and reasoned thoughts;
- heart – your emotional response.

Here you can consider how this made you feel, e.g. were you puzzled, shocked, angry, confused, saddened, happy, etc.?

Analysis

Looking back, consider the component parts that made up the experience. For example, if you are writing about a situation, who was involved, what issues, problems, topics, existed? Was the time of day significant? What went together to create the situation? Were there any prominent underlying factors? Had this been going on for quite a while? If the experience was a course or meeting you were involved with, what did you learn?

Interpretation

Ask yourself, what does this mean to you? Where do you fit in to the big picture? Are you happy with this? Do you want anything to change? If you are faced with a problem, think about the experience, what can be changed, what is possible? Is it you, the organisation, the environment, a combination of two or three factors? Realistically, what can be done, if anything? How has this experience changed your outlook? If the experience was a course or meeting, how does what you learned sit with what you already know? What are the implications to you, your students or the organisation?

Action plan

What will I do differently in future? Remember the importance of being SMART.

Time allocated to this task

Consider how much time this professional reflective practice has taken. That is not just the time it has taken to record your thoughts but the time allocated to you conducting the appropriate activity and thinking around the subject.

Total time

Keep a running count of the total time allocated towards a total of 30 hours (or pro-rata) CPD.

If this is your first attempt at writing your entry, we suggest that you restrict yourself to the subjects listed above within the pro forma. Like most things, when you begin it may require a lot of concentration and it could be a relatively slow process. However, what is important is that you are actually doing it.

As you practise professional reflective practice you may feel that you are ready to consider more aspects in relation to any given experience. For this we offer the following pro forma in the series of three.

Professional Reflective Practice Account Pro forma 2 (PRP2)

Date..

Nature of experience: S, C, O, P, E, Other...

An overview of the experience	
My reaction	
My analysis	
My connections	
My reading	
My professional practice	
My interpretation	
My action plan	
Time allocated to this task	Total time

This pro forma is designed to move your reflective practice on to include a richer variety of considerations or topics. You can begin at this stage if you feel able. Here the reaction and analysis remain the same but included are reference to connections, reading and professional practice.

Connections

What is meant by 'connections' are the associations to other experiences in your professional capacity. Here you are attempting to identify similarities and differences between this and other events or encounters. You are looking for patterns, in yourself, in others and within organisations.

Reading

Like connections above, the reading section enables you to consider your studies and identify any links to theory. Often what we have witnessed, experienced or heard about has been thought about and written about by others. Their own opinions, views, observations and insights can very often help us to understand our own unique situation.

Professional practice

This considers what links can be made to your own professional practice. If for example you have attended an in-house course, or are studying for a qualification, it would be pertinent to make any links between this and your professional practice. It doesn't have to have a huge impact and in fact you could consider the experience in terms of what you will not do, as well as identifying what may be useful for your own practice. The last boxes 'Interpretation', 'Action plan' and 'Time' have been considered previously.

Once you are proficient at this stage there are a few more considerations that are considered pertinent. These are included within the final pro forma shown below.

Professional Reflective Practice Account Pro forma 3 (PRP3)

Date...

Nature of Experience: S, C, O, P, E, Other..

A brief overview of the experience	
Reason for undertaking this activity	
Reaction	
Analysis	
Interpretation	
Connections	
Reading	
Knowledge, skills, attitude	
Professional practice	
Impact assessment	
Action plan	
Time allocated to this task	Total time

The above pro forma seeks to guide you through the considerations to ensure you are capturing all aspects of a situation, incident or event. Only the boxes that have not yet been described are considered here, with the exception of the experience.

A brief overview of the experience

You will notice that all that is being asked for here is a brief overview. This is because if writing is very descriptive it is likely to be less reflective. This will be discussed in the next chapter, which considers levels of reflective practice.

Reason for undertaking this activity

This asks the question, why did I do this? There can be many reasons why you engage in any activity. Sometimes we volunteer because we want to participate, on other occasions we volunteer because it gets us out of doing something else that we don't want to do. Whatever the reason for doing something, the most difficult experience is to undertake an activity because we have to. The child in us will rebel, whereas the adult in us will find ways of making the experience pleasurable and advantageous.

Knowledge, skills, attitude

This considers the acquisition of knowledge and skills gained from any activity and your associated attitude. Knowledge and skills are generally easy to assess; however, your attitude is less easy to determine. You, though, are in an ideal situation to judge your own attitude. New experiences and sharing ideas with others can have a bearing upon your attitude. Perhaps your activity involved meeting people from a very different background to your own and you suddenly realised that you had paid them scant thought or recognition. Perhaps you were placed in a position where decisions had to be made and you found that you were making those decisions whereas until that time you retreated from such a role. Often it is some time after an event that we realise that we think or behave differently than we did before.

Impact assessment

Having considered all the previous aspects, you are then in a position to assess what impact the experience has had upon you in your professional capacity.

How much should be written?

The answer to this question is very much dependent upon your attitude towards professional reflective practice. We suggest that if you buy into the concept, it will reap rewards. On the other hand, if you choose to do the minimum possible then that is your choice. There are no hard-and-fast rules in relation to word counts at this stage. However, as teachers/lecturers we all have a shrewd idea of the amount of effort given to a piece of work. Thirty hours (or pro-rata) CPD is expected from you each year. If you chose to spend one day in every month engaged in CPD then you would spend 2 hours and 30 minutes per month. If you spread the 30 hours over a period of once a week then you would need to spend 34.6 minutes per week; doing it each day of the year will take you just over 5 minutes.

How often should I reflect?

This depends on your circumstances at the time. If you were to engage in CPD twice in a month then that would give you 1¼ hours on task. This time would enable you to get into the subject in a meaningful way. It is recognised that people's lives cannot be regulated nicely into slots of time allocated for specific tasks – reality creeps in and things are put on hold sometimes as a necessity. Try though to set a certain time aside for your professional reflective practice, because getting into the habit of doing something means that you are more likely to complete your task, and you will benefit from the momentum of the activity.

Can I do too much?

The 30 hours (or pro-rata), are the minimum expected from the Institute for Learning (IfL). If you are enjoying what you do and find it assists you professionally as well as on a personal level, than that is fine. Like anything, taking it to excess is possibly not good for you.

What can I not write about?

Within reason and provided you do not break the law you can write about any topic you wish. The IfL, and your employer, may ask to see your CPD portfolio, but otherwise unless you choose to share what you have written with other people, it will remain private. You are a professional and so a professional approach to your CPD entry would be appropriate. For instance, use initials rather than names of people, especially if you wish to comment upon situations that are becoming heated.

How will this affect me as a manager?

An advantage of the Reflect system is that it lends itself to a more uniform approach to the management of CPD. Managers who are responsible for their staff believe that at the end of each year it will help give them a much better idea of what's happening. Watkinson, (2008) from the Centre of Excellence in Leadership recognises that *It will be possible for CPD managers to capture a whole range of formal and informal CPD that has taken place in the organisation and to evaluate not only what has taken place but what impact that has had*.

What format should I use for my CPD entry?

It does not matter which format you choose. However, if you want to ensure your writing is reflective rather than descriptive, form PRP3 above should assist your writing. The following chapter offers further advice in relation to your writing and importantly the level of your reflective practice, but this does not necessarily affect the format. If you prefer, you can visit the IfL website and use their purpose-built software, Reflect.

I have heard about Reflect on the IfL website, what does it do?

According to the Institute for Learning website:

> *Reflect is an online system which incorporates a range of tools to help you plan, record, reflect on and evidence your Continuing Professional Development (CPD) activity.*

> (IfL, 2008)

The use of information technology in general will be discussed before identifying the benefits of adopting Reflect.

The use of information technology

The use of information technology (IT) is growing exponentially. According to the BBC (2008), since 2002, personal computer and laptop use has grown fourfold. In fact in 2007 the average person in the UK spent 24 minutes per day on their computer and 36 per cent of adults use the internet every day. Research into this trend by Ofcom (2008) which focused on trends and developments in the UK's communications market reported that by the end of 2003, there were nearly 3 million broadcast connections. Five years later, around 60 per cent of households (15 million) have a broadband connection. For many, IT is inescapable; it has permeated our work, social and personal lives. The full extent of its influence is often noticed during times of its unexpected absence: for those working on a computer, when the system shuts down then so do we. We buy, research, communicate, play, work and study online. There is no opt-out for those quite happy to use a pen and paper. It has become apparent that IT is here to stay, it moves quickly and we must try to keep up with it.

At times it can feel that we are always just lagging behind, as today's terminology is quickly surpassed by the new wizardry which is described using the latest technical nouns; a language that you may suspect is intentionally exclusionary in nature. As you learn all about your new up-to-date Bluetooth application, someone suggests you would have been better off with a Zigbee; how quickly it changes and how easily we can become despondent. But the latest research supports the suggestion that many people are keeping up with the changes. According to Ofcom:

> Over a quarter of internet users in April 2008 were aged 35–49 – broadly in line with the proportion of the UK population – but they only accounted for 17% of time spent online in the same month. The age groups which accounted for a greater share of time spent online include 18–24s, 25–34s and 50–64 year olds. 18–34 year olds use the internet particularly intensively – they accounted for 23% of the population but 36% of all internet use.

> (Ofcom, 2008, page 129)

These data indicate that in relation to age, many are able to use the internet and therefore by implication are computer literate. But what about the gender divide; is the adoption of IT skills predominantly favoured by one gender in particular? According to Ofcom (2008), men and women spend roughly equal amounts of time online. However, there is a variation noted by virtue of age. Women aged 25–34 and 35–49 account for approximately 55 per cent of the time spent online by these total age groups, whereas men account for over 70 per cent of the time spent online by the over-65s.

The statistics are interesting and to an extent useful, but what they do not tell us about are those remaining with no IT skills or those who are lagging behind. For example, what are their IT needs, what do they require to perform adequately? This book makes no assumptions as to your level of knowledge and explains IT in terms that is accessible to the average Lizard; a would be computer Wizard who Lacks Information; wizard – lizard. As a computer Lizard you are aware that there is much to be learned, fully accepting of this situation, willing to learn and quite capable. The beauty of any system that changes very quickly, such as IT, is that it doesn't matter if you have not kept up to date with recent changes, you can always catch up. You don't need to know how something works to be able to use it; you just need to understand the instructions that come with it. Therein lies the problem: if we can't understand the terminology, we can't use the available IT. Take for example the term 'WebFolio'; the word 'web' and the word 'folio' are perfectly understandable, but the two words placed together could make no sense unless they are explained (they will be explained fully later in this chapter). It may be worth considering some of the more common terminology employed within the world of IT.

Common terminology used within IT

Have you ever read something and although you were able to recognise and speak the words, you found that as a whole they made absolutely no sense to you whatsoever? This phenomenon can be experienced for example when reading about the latest IT gadgetry. For some, this experience can hamper your enjoyment of IT. Some of the advantages of IT can be lost to the lay person; the authors included. For many of us, the benefits of IT are missed behind words that have little or no meaning. As a consequence, the advantages of new and very useful IT systems are lost not so much 'in translation' but due to the lack of it. We are simply not aware of the meaning of some of the terminology being used. As a consequence the terminology employed from this point in the book will be translated in a more descriptive manner.

Those who have studied IT appreciate the need to adopt new words. For example, Sutherland (2008) observes that, *I've also learned a whole new technical vocabulary, in some context I almost sound like a geek*. But like any jargon, technical terminology is used by way of a short cut to describe a concept, procedure or as a suitable noun. At the end of this chapter we offer some jargon-busting explanations in the form of a glossary. If you feel that you are familiar with these terms, a direction to further reading is offered within References and further reading.

The Institute for Learning's Reflect

Reflect is designed specifically for teachers in further education. According to IfL, it is an education cyberspace where teachers can record their thoughts and experiences and obtain support for their CPD. Davies, (2008) from the IfL observed that:

> We didn't want a dry eportfolio in which they just collected a huge volume of evidence. We wanted something that would support them in their teaching and also that provided them with a platform for secure online learning.

Reflect was first introduced to the IfL as a piece of software called PebblePad designed by Pebble Learning. According to Pebble Learning, PebblePad was a response to UK Higher Education's need to provide opportunities for personal development planning (PDP) to its students. Paper-based systems were considered to be costly, inefficient and failed to 'excite' users. Pebble Learning was already creating e-learning tools and materials while the two directors, Shane Sutherland and Colin Dalziel, still worked at the University of Wolverhampton. All of the employees of Pebble Learning are graduates of the university. According to Sutherland (2008):

> We developed (and enhanced) two of our existing tools into a single system called PebblePad. Uniquely amongst 'eportfolio' systems PebblePad provided scaffolding for recording common user experiences/needs (action plans; meeting records; reflective thoughts; experiences). We also put the user at the centre of the experience; kept the space absolutely private and allowed the user to share 'assets' with people they trusted or needed to share with. This meant that users could record a wide range of experiences within and beyond Uni' and share them with tutors; friends; employers; family etc.

> (Sutherland, 2008)

Pebble Learning emphasise that it was the strong pedagogic principles and reflective nature of their system and the fact it is user-friendly that meant that it was quickly adopted by a number of universities. As a result it came to the attention of the IfL. Sutherland (2008) recalls that, *When we described its principles to the IfL they felt that the tool was sympathetic to their needs. They asked us to make a few changes and adopted it as Reflect*. It was trialled in January 2008 and it went live to all IfL members on 8 April. To date it has about 8,000 users.

There are many advantages of using Reflect over a paper document. For example, you can share information with others all over the world and receive feedback and supporting comments. But the advantages go further than just information sharing and feedback; it is possible to link items together, access information from any networked computer – a networked computer is that which is connected to the internet. Further benefits include the use of tags (labels), things to make it easy to aggregate items (the act of collecting things under various tags). Links can be created to other items on the web and data can be reused from the membership database. Learning journals can be created and maintained very easily. Work can be peer-reviewed without photocopying and posting across the UK and as a result our carbon footprint will be reduced.

The CPD activities that the system offers include:

- recording thoughts about how a lesson went;
- planning an activity;
- drawing up an action plan;
- setting up a web portfolio or a blog;
- reflecting on a wide range of experiences, e.g. teaching.

The information recorded on Reflect is private, that is unless you give your specific permission for others to share it. Having done this, it can be distributed to colleagues, other professionals and friends or can simply be used as an *aide-mémoire*. The beauty of this system is that it provides a handy mechanism for you to submit a record of your CPD activity to the IfL. The IfL's Reflect e-portfolio is user-friendly, takes very little time to get accustomed to and as a tool for recording you professional reflective practice is ideal. We will now consider some of the activities available to you within Reflect.

Activities available within Reflect

Reflect offers a variety of activities to assist with your CPD. When these are completed you end up with a record stored within the account of the owner. These records are collectively known as 'assets'; this term has been adopted because of the value they have for you. Those most commonly used activities are Action plan, Activities, Meetings, Thoughts, Abilities, Achievements and Experiences. These will be considered in turn and are reproduced in part with kind permission from Pebble Learning Ltd and the Institute for Learning.

Action plan

This allows you to create action plans which are designed to help you achieve a particular outcome or goal. Action plans are written by learners to help them improve what they are currently able to do or as part of an activity planning process. The action plan tool includes what is referred to as a 'steps to success' function where larger goals are be broken down into smaller steps. Further, a SWOT analysis section is included.

Activities

The activity asset allows you to record any event or experience; for example, a workshop or training course you have attended, a conference you presented at or a project you have been involved in. You can record any activity which you think might be useful in the future. This may be as part of a CPD record for appraisal or simply so you can privately review things you are involved in. Activity records are likely to provide useful evidence towards your overall development record; for appraisal review as well as providing a record that you can return to review upon your progress. You may find that recording your ongoing activities helps you to identify future development goals.

Meetings

The meetings activity allows you to record significant meetings you have had with other people such as module tutors, personal tutors, careers advisers or with fellow students working on projects. Like action plans, meetings include a facility for recording the outcomes of meetings and for planning how and when the outcomes will be addressed. You can also create a meeting record in advance of a meeting and edit it afterwards to reflect revised outcomes and actions required.

Thoughts

The thought activity enables you to record thoughts and reflections on any event or experience of significance to you. Thinking about how, why and where you learn is an important aspect of learning, which is why every record type has a section called 'Reflecting on learning'. Thoughts provide an input record which is concerned with learning from experience. Many courses and professional vocations place great value in personal and professional reflection and the recording of thoughts may prove very useful later if you are required to provide evidence of your reflective practice. Thought records are also automatically created when you add a new entry to a blog (referred to later).

Abilities

Here you can record abilities, skills, competencies and other attributes which you feel are significant or which are required by an external agency for the purposes of assessment, accreditation or validation. You can describe your ability, skill or competency in your own words or copy an official description of your attributes being recorded.

Achievements

Here you record any successful endeavour which is significant to you. The achievement recorded here does not have to relate to an academic course; indeed, many achievements will be related to sporting, cultural or social pursuits. Because potential employers are interested in what people do outside of their academic courses you should record any achievement which may be useful in the future.

Experiences

The experience activity allows you to record any event of experience which is relevant to you, for example, a particular role, a series of activities that made up a broader experience, a project you have been involved in, or any other general experience not appropriate to record as Ability, Achievement, Meeting or Thought.

Other activities within Reflect

Blogs
Blogs are single-page websites which tend to contain a chronological account of a person's experiences (blog is short for 'weblog'). Blogs are often created as personal journals which are regularly updated by the creator. Normally blogs are automatically made public, but blogs in Reflect are confidential to you, unless you choose to share them with others.

Blogs can be used for many things, for example, as a CPD journal to provide material for further reflection, as a project diary, to keep track of progress on placements or how working with a particular group is progressing. Blogs are valuable tools in someone's learning journey and have been designed in such a way that they can be created, published and shared in the same way as all other assets, or they can be added as integral parts of a WebFolio. Entries made to a blog can also be saved as individual 'Thoughts' and entries made using the thoughts input can be published directly to a blog.

Proforma
Proforma are blank templates which you can fill in and which save to your Reflect. You may be asked to complete a proforma for a particular activity or for a particular purpose. Just like all standard Reflect assets, once you have completed a proforma it can be saved, shared and linked within Reflect and you can attach other files to it.

Special types of activities

The WebFolio and CPD record are special types of asset which can be used to collate other types of asset to build a representative record of your activities. These are described below.

WebFolio
A WebFolio is a website containing a collection of your records and files which are selected and drawn together for a particular purpose to present 'stories' about yourself and about your activities. It is as easy to create as all of the other assets, offers the user a wide choice of templates, colour schemes and image options to create your own evidence-based website. You can choose any number of pages which are named according to preference. Like all 'assets', the WebFolios can be shared, copied, duplicated and edited at will. This means that if you are applying for several different jobs you could create multiple custom WebFolios to meet the specific needs of the different potential employers. Pages may also contain links to websites and other assets within Reflect.

CPD record
The CPD record enables you to bring together items you would like to use to demonstrate your CPD activity during a given period. They display as a single page that lists entries made to them in date order. You can send any normal asset from your Reflect asset store to your CPD record except files such as WebFolios, blogs and CVs. You can create multiple CPD records for different purposes such as appraisal and of course your IfL annual CPD return. When you select a CPD record you can select it for submission to the IfL. The IfL CPD record will display the number of hours you are required to complete for your annual CPD cycle. As you add items to the CPD record you will also see how many hours you have completed, so you can easily gauge how you are progressing. Once you have completed the required number of hours you can send your CPD return straight to the IfL from Reflect.

Tags

Tags are the things that allow you to group together your assets to enable you to quickly locate items, cross-reference records, and identify areas of activity and to aggregate items quickly. Any assets can be tagged using pre-defined tags or tags created by the user. The pre-defined tags are Institutional context, Learning and teaching and Subject specialism. These tags embody the three most important areas that your CPD should address. Tags provide a means of organising assets within the e-portfolio store but can also be used for instant publishing. Users can choose to publish any of their tags as a WebFolio page. PebblePad automatically orders the assets by creation date and displays them by title and description.

The following is a summary of the assets in Reflect.

Asset	A record of a completed activity within Reflect which can be:

- **Action plan**   Skills, competencies, abilities you want to plan for
- **Activity**   Records specific CPD activity
- **Meeting**   Records meetings with others
- **Thought**   Records thoughts and reflections
- **Ability**   Records your skills, competencies or abilities
- **Achievements** Records your achievements
- **Experience**   Record your personal or professional experience

Blog	A tool for creating an online journal diary
Proforma	Tailored forms for your course or profession
WebFolio	An evidence-based web-publishing system where you can publish things to other people across the internet
Tags	Tags are the things that allow you to group together your assets
CPD record	A record of items brought together to demonstrate continuing professional development activity

There are many more features contained within Reflect, but to explain them out of context would achieve little as IT often involves a skill and therefore it is more appropriate to do it rather than to read about it.

TASK TASK **TASK** TASK **TASK** TASK TASK **TASK** TASK **TASK** **TASK** TASK

We recommend that you visit the IfL website and try out the Reflect package for yourself.

A SUMMARY OF **KEY POINTS**

In this chapter we have considered the following key points.

> Identifying an appropriate structure for your reflective writing employing the mnemonic SCOPE and offering a set of three incremental pro formas.

> Stating the characteristics and indicative content of three pro formas resulting in the use of the following headings: a brief overview of the experience, reason for undertaking this activity, reaction, analysis, interpretation connections, reading, knowledge, skills, attitude, professional practice, impact assessment and action plan.

> Explaining the range and extent of your CPD activity and identifying frequently asked questions and answers.

> Recognising the supporting role of information technology drawing upon the Ofcom report in relation to the use of IT within the UK and identifying trends in IT use over the last five years.

> Demystifying common IT terminology and offering a jargon-buster to assist understanding of common IT terminology.

> Identifying the activities available within Institute for Learning's Reflect software package and providing an overview of its functions, describing some of the activities available to the user.

REFERENCES AND FURTHER READING REFERENCES AND FURTHER READING

BBC News spending on communications falls: http://news.bbc.co.uk/1/hi/technology/7559557.stm. Accessed 14 August 2008.

Davies, L (2008) Reflect CD-ROM. Institute for Learning.

Institute for Learning (2008) www.ifl.ac.uk. Accessed 12 August 2008.

Ofcom (Office of Communications). Communications Market Report 2008 www.ofcom.org.uk/research/cm/cmr08/cmr08_1.pdf. Accessed 14 August 2008.

Storm, J (2008) *What did he say? Computer jargon explained.* http://www.jonstorm.com/glossary/glosssz.htm. Accessed 14 August 2008.

Sutherland, S (2008) www.pebblelearning.co.uk. Accessed 23 October 2008.

Carolyn Watkinson (2008) *Help with computer jargon and terminology.* From the Centre of Excellence in Leadership Supanet.com Help (2008) www.supanet.com/help/help_computer_jargon/news/30835/Computer_jargon:_A-E.html. Accessed 14 August 2008.

7
Levels of reflective writing

By the end of this chapter you will be able to:

- explain different levels of reflective writing as described by the three frameworks referred to;
- identify the characteristics of each level of reflective writing;
- describe how to develop a reflective account to the next level;
- critically evaluate your own writing, identifying how to improve it.

Professional Standards

This chapter relates to the following Professional Standards.

Professional Values:

AS 4 Reflection and evaluation of their own practice and their continuing professional development as teachers.

Professional Knowledge and Understanding:

AK 4.3 Ways to reflect, evaluate and use research to develop own practice, and to share good practice with others.

Professional Practice:

AP 4.2 Reflect on and demonstrate commitment to improvement of own personal and teaching skills through regular evaluation and use of feedback.

AP 4.3 Share good practice with others and engage in continuing professional development through reflection, evaluation and the appropriate use of research.

Introduction

Chapter 5 gave you some examples of a range of activities you can undertake that may count towards your CPD requirements. Chapter 6 offered pro formas and structure, making links to the IfL's Reflect. This chapter introduces different levels of reflective writing, giving an overview of some of the literature. It further gives examples of reflective writing and offers guidance, for you to write at these levels yourself. As Moon (2004, page 96) explains, the use of the term 'levels of reflection' implies a hierarchy. Reflection and reflective writing range from the superficial, very descriptive writing, reporting what happened, to the highly analytical and questioning, profound, deep levels of reflective writing. In the literature a number of writers have tried to identify the characteristics of these different levels of reflection. The purpose of this is that by identifying the characteristics, and the associated level, you can assess your current level of reflection, identify how to improve and move to the next level.

Levels of reflective writing

Hatton and Smith (1995) identified a framework for four types of writing. The first one is non-reflective, while the other three are characterised as different kinds of reflection (the examples are Hatton and Smith's).

- Descriptive writing (not reflective) reports events that occurred or is a report of something you have read in the literature. There is no attempt to provide reasons or justifications for the events. Its main purpose is to provide a support or a starting point for the framework.
- Descriptive reflection attempts to provide reasons and justifications for events or actions but in a reportive, or descriptive way. Although there is some recognition of alternate viewpoints, it is mainly based upon personal judgement, e.g., *I chose this problem-solving activity because I believe the learners should be active rather than passive*.
- Dialogic reflection demonstrates a 'stepping back' from the events/actions leading to a different level of mulling about discourse with one's self through the exploration of possible reasons, e.g., *I became aware that a number of students did not respond to written text materials. Thinking about this, there may have been several reasons. A number of students may still have lacked some confidence in handling the level of language in the text.*
- Critical reflection demonstrates an awareness that actions and events are explained by multiple perspectives. It involves giving reasons for decisions or events, which takes into account the broader historical, social and/or political contexts, e.g., *What must be recognised, however, is that the issues of student management experienced with this class can only be understood within the wider structural locations of power relationships established between teachers and students in schools as social institutions based upon the principle of control.*

Hatton and Smith (1995) explain that their framework indicates a perceived developmental sequence. It is likely that you move on from the non-reflective, descriptive writing to descriptive reflection, becoming more able to give a range of reasons for acting as you did. As you become increasingly aware of the problematic nature of professional action, you begin a rather exploratory and tentative examination of why things occur the way they do, here termed dialogic reflection. Finally, the use of critical perspectives depends on the development of metacognitive (or thinking about thinking) skills alongside a grasp and acceptance of particular ideological frameworks.

How do you move from one level of reflective writing to the next? In their research, Hatton and Smith (1995) identified that a significant strategy in facilitating the development of reflection is the use of 'critical friend' dyads. In these dyads, you engage one-to-one with a colleague or other person, who acts as a 'critical friend', in a way which encourages you to talk openly, being questioned or even confronted, in order to examine your CPD activities or teaching practice, in terms of planning decisions, delivery and evaluation. In these dyads you are able to distance yourself from your actions, ideas and beliefs, holding them up for scrutiny in the company of a peer with whom you are willing to take such risks. Therefore, an element of trust is required. As stated by Hatton and Smith (1995), it creates an opportunity for giving voice to one's own thinking while at the same time being heard in a sympathetic but constructively critical way. The dyads can be reciprocal; you can be your colleague's critical friend. Alternatively, the whole process can be more collaborative in nature, where all members of a team or department are involved. Small groups can take on the role of critical friend, to widen the perspective. Some of you may be reluctant to share information and open yourself for feedback. Therefore, the meetings should take place in a safe environment where no one is worried about being ridiculed and feedback is constructive. To be of most benefit, time needs to be allocated for the meetings. Although coincidental meetings in the corridor, just before or after a teaching session, can be helpful, a structured slot on the timetable will ensure that all members of the team are involved, developing their reflective skills.

Hatton and Smith (1995) further recognise that certain language patterns and syntax are likely to ensure a more reflective approach. This is particularly relevant to the dialogic level of reflective writing. As defined, this kind of reflecting involves stepping back from, mulling over, or tentatively exploring reasons. The following examples (from Hatton and Smith) of language construction can help you achieve the dialogic level.

... This was quite possibly due to ... Alternatively,...

...The problem here, I believe, was the fact that...

...While it may be true that...

...On the one hand, ..., yet on the other...

...In thinking back, ... On reflection, ...

...I guess that ... has made me aware of...

Based on the above, Moon (2004, page 214) developed a *generic framework for reflective writing*, which has the following four categories.

Descriptive writing	Some references to emotional reactions but they are not explored and not related to behaviour Account relates to ideas or external information Little attempt to focus on particular issues Hardly reflective at all
Descriptive account with some reflection	Descriptive with little addition of external ideas, some reference to alternative viewpoints Some notion of asking questions but no response, i.e. no analysis Sense of recognition that learning can be gained from the event
Reflective writing (1)	There is description but it's focused with particular aspects accentuated Evidence of external ideas Some analysis Willingness to be critical of the action, self or others Some 'standing back' from the event Different perspectives are considered
Reflective writing (2)	Description now only serves to set the context Clear 'standing back' Self-questioning evident, critical self-awareness Views and motives of others are taken into account, multiple perspectives Recognition that events exist in a historical or social context Observation that there is learning to be gained Recognition that personal frame of reference can change according to emotional state

Samuels (2008) has devised a model for self-assessment of reflective writing, which is based on a five-point scale developed by Bain et al. In this model, the levels of reflective writing start with Reporting, which is not reflective and is similar to Hatton and Smith's first level. The next level is Responding, where feelings are described. The focus is on the self, without any justifications. Thirdly is Relating, where links are started to get formed. The next step is Reasoning. You are making links to other experiences and theory. You are starting to question and analyse, seeing things from other perspectives. Finally, in Restructuring, you look at the wider picture, draw your own informed conclusions, taking control.

Reporting	Describing what happened without adding any observations
Responding	Describing feelings Making observations but without discussing the reason for these observations Reflecting within your own frameworks of thinking Reflecting about particular situations and events Working with the particular and personal Greater focus on your own practice
Relating	Linking what happened to personal experience Recognising what you do well and what you need to develop, what you have learned Identifying action plans and ways to develop practice Identifying why something has happened – without any in-depth analysis
Reasoning	Linking what happened to other experiences, to theory and concepts in order to assimilate and accommodate Analysing, questioning, seeking answers Looking for alternatives, putting forward your own ideas Actively seeking to understand and explain how and why Generalising Making connections between theory and practice – using theory to make sense of practice Testing out theory Seeing from other perspectives, challenging your own perspective Questioning
Reconstructing	High-level abstract thinking to draw out general conclusions and apply learning Drawing your own conclusions Developing your own theories Making a decision about what you believe – values, theories, models of practice Taking control of your own learning, recognising and acting on the personal significance of your learning
Plans to develop my reflective journal writing – what is my next step? What am I ready to develop?	

To develop your writing, it is helpful to read back one of your reflective entries and judge where on the scale it fits most accurately. It doesn't matter which of the frameworks or models you use; use the one that you feel you can relate to best. Alternatively, ask a 'critical friend' to look at your work for an honest and constructive opinion. Your next step is to look at the characteristics of the next level and rewrite your entry to incorporate those character-istics. As stated by Moon (2004), you need to take care not to reject all descriptive writing. Some description is necessary as a starting point, to provide background to the reflection, to set the scene.

Where and when does the reflection stop? Moon (2004, page 98) points out: *logically, there is no 'end-point' of reflection – it can go on and on examining issues in a wider and wider context.* However, you need to be practical. You may have been given a maximum word count for your reflective entry. It makes sense, therefore, to stay focused on your practice rather than allowing yourself to get too deeply immersed in socio-political issues.

The next part of this chapter gives some examples of different levels of reflective writing. Read the following.

Presentation skills workshop 1

Yesterday, I attended a workshop on presentation skills. Although I'm new to teaching, I have given some presentations to my colleagues in my previous job. However, I've always found this a scary experience. The trainers seemed to know what they were doing, and from paper, seemed well qualified. They seemed approachable and genuinely interested in what our expectations, fears, wants, etc., were. In fact, these were talked about and put onto a flipchart. They went through all the health and safety regulations, such as fire escape and meeting point, toilets, etc. Then, the session started properly. After everybody introduced themselves, we were asked to write down a topic, these were then mixed together and we had to choose one. Next, we had to stand in front of the class and talk about the subject we had been given for two minutes. I was nervous at first but then as I got started it became easier. I don't think anyone actually managed to do exactly two minutes, most of us ran over for some reason. After this we discussed things like what makes a good teacher, bad teacher, or experiences at school, techniques and being prepared. I don't know why, but we were given a test which identified whether we were a visual, auditory or kinaesthetic learner. I thought most in the class would be visual, but it turned out to be more or less equal auditory and visual; there were lots of feelings/doing people in the class.

Where the time actually went I don't know, but after lunch we really got going. We were put into small groups where we had to prepare a five-minute presentation, which only one of us from each group had to present. I didn't actually do any of the presenting. The day was OK, at least it was a break from teaching. Most people seemed to moan a bit about having to do too much in the workshop. After all, the trainers are paid to run it, let them earn their money!

TASK TASK **TASK** TASK **TASK** **TASK** TASK **TASK** TASK **TASK** **TASK** TASK

Looking at the five-point scale described above, where do you think this piece of writing fits best? How can the author develop their writing to bring it to the next level?

This first piece of writing is mainly at the Reporting level with some elements of the Reporting level, or, in terms of Hatton and Smith, at the Descriptive writing level. To bring the writing up to the next level, the author has to provide some reasons and justifications for what happened, reflect on strengths and weaknesses and recognise what has been learned.

Presentation skills workshop 2

Yesterday, I attended a workshop on presentation skills. Although I'm new to teaching, I have given some presentations to my colleagues in my previous job. However, I've always found this a scary experience. This is probably because I don't feel comfortable being the centre of attention. I worry that I may blush or stumble over my words. The trainers seemed to know what they were doing, and from paper, seemed well qualified. They seemed approachable and genuinely interested in what our expectations, fears, wants, etc., were. In fact, these were talked about and put onto a flipchart. They went through all the health and safety regulations, such as fire escape and meeting point, toilets, etc. Then, the session started properly. After everybody introduced themselves, we were asked to write down a topic, these were then mixed together and we had to choose one. Next, we had to stand in front of the class and talk about the subject we had been given for two minutes. I was nervous at first but then as I got started it became easier. Perhaps this was because I actually knew a bit about the subject. I don't think anyone managed to do exactly two minutes, most of us ran over because we hadn't anticipated people asking questions about the presentation. I will remember this when I'm in class. After this we discussed things like what makes a good teacher, bad teacher, or experiences at school, techniques and being prepared. We were given a test which identified our preferred learning style: visual, auditory or kinaesthetic. I thought most in the class would be visual, but it turned out to be more or less equal auditory and visual; there were lots of feelings/doing people in the class.

Where the time actually went I don't know, but after lunch we really got going. We were put into small groups where we had to prepare a five-minute presentation, which only one of us from each group would present. I didn't actually do any of the presenting but I learned a lot about what preparation actually entails. The one thing I will remember about this workshop is 'fail to prepare, prepare to fail' and I don't want to do that.

Although the day wasn't what I expected, it was beneficial. I think that most people assumed that we would be told how to present rather than doing it ourselves. It's called experiential learning I believe. When some people didn't get what they expected, they started moaning. I have learned from this as well. Whenever I am involved in a workshop, I will be ensuring that everybody knows the purpose of the day and will be informed of exactly what to expect.

As you notice, the content of the account hasn't changed a great deal but it is more reflective now. It gives some reasons and justifications for events, some other viewpoints or perspectives and there is some recognition of what has been learned from the experience.

The next two reflective accounts develop from the Relating level to the Reasoning level; or from the Descriptive reflection to Dialogic reflection, Reflective writing 1 in Moon (2004).

TASK TASK **TASK** TASK **TASK** **TASK** TASK **TASK** TASK **TASK** **TASK** TASK

Compare the two accounts and identify, by underlining, which aspects classify the second account as Reasoning/dialogic level.

Teaching IT in a young offenders establishment 1

What I hoped to achieve from the course was an understanding of web design and how I could use it in the workshop to help motivate and provide a challenge to all students of all different abilities. I also hoped that it could be a fun lesson and that the students would be able to see their work progressing quickly.

I completed the course which I had found interesting but had not realised how tough it was going to be. I fully expected that it would be a matter of putting together a few pictures and a few words and that a web page would miraculously appear. In doing the course I soon realised that there is a lot more to web design and that it is a very complicated and precise procedure. We had started the course with HTML and how it works with producing a web page. This was very difficult as you had to remember different tags. These are key words or phrases enclosed in angle brackets < >. The words or phrases describe how text and images should be displayed and how links can be created. This was a very difficult part of the course to do as there was a lot to remember.

We then went on to use Photoshop. For this we were asked to go around the local village and take pictures. After we had taken our photographs we transferred them on to our

computer to organise and rename them. We selected some to edit, retouch and repair, then saved images in different file format. Again interesting and fun to play around with but it is very technical and would need a lot of time spent on perfecting and getting the end results required.

I thought the course was very interesting and very informative and I certainly learnt a lot. It also made me realise how complicated it was going to be to introduce web design into the workshop. Looking at course worksheets on the OCR site, I realised that we would not be able to use the briefs of assignments that were available. Therefore we were going to have to set up an assignment that would be workable within our own workshop and our environment and also to follow the criteria set for OCR. It was decided to do a web design that could be shown as a presentation in induction for when young men and young adults first come into the establishment. The idea is to show the various courses available in the workshops and the qualifications that are on offer.

Students are not allowed to walk around the establishment taking pictures. Also, if pictures are taken within the workshops, no faces can be seen so that people are not recognised. Also we cannot make the course too long as students do not stop here very long.

The course was tried in the workshop and it was a course that the students wanted to do. It started with explaining HTML and how it works. This worked fine if students came to every session, but this doesn't happen very often in this environment. We then found that at every session we had to repeat one or two of the sessions that we had previously covered. This was making it difficult to keep the lessons flowing. It was decided that it might be easier to offer the course to a few students at a time and let them work in small groups. This way different groups would be at different levels to complete the necessary coursework and as students come and go there would still be some in the workshop that would be progressing towards completing the coursework.

Teaching IT in a young offenders establishment 2

What I hoped to achieve from the course was an understanding of web design and how I could use it in the workshop to help motivate and provide a challenge to all students of all different abilities. According to the literature, students are more motivated when lessons are fun and when students see their work progressing quickly. This is especially important in our establishment, as students tend to move on quickly.

I have attended other courses, which I found really interesting and useful, just pitched at the right level for me. This course, although I completed it, was more difficult than I expected it to be. I fully expected that it would be a matter of putting together a few pictures and a few words and that a web page would miraculously appear. In doing the course I soon realised that there is a lot more to web design and that it is a very complicated and precise procedure. It might have been helpful to me if I had attended the 'Introduction to Web Design' first. I will suggest this to other colleagues who also want to go on the course. We had started the course with HTML and how it works with producing a web page. This was very difficult as you had to remember different tags. These are key words or phrases enclosed in angle brackets < >. The words or phrases describe how text and images should be displayed and how links can be created. This was a very difficult part of the course as there was a lot to remember. Normally I'm quite good at remembering things, but these concepts are so abstract, that I found it hard. This is something I must remember for my own students. Perhaps I can look into the use of a mnemonic or something, to help them.

We then went on to use Photoshop. For this we were asked to go around the local village and take pictures. After we had taken our photographs we transferred them on to our computer to organise and rename them. We selected some to edit, retouch and repair, then saved images in different file format. Again interesting and fun to play around with but it is very technical and would need a lot of time spent on perfecting and getting the end results required.

I thought the course was very interesting and very informative and I certainly learnt a lot. It also made me realise how complicated it was going to be to introduce web design into the workshop. It was decided to do a web design that could be shown as a presentation in induction for when young men and young adults first come into the establishment. The idea is to show the various courses available in the workshops and the qualifications that are on offer.

Students are not allowed to walk around the establishment taking pictures. Also, if pictures are taken within the workshops, no faces can be seen so that people are not recognised. Also we cannot make the course too long as students do not stop here very long.

The course was tried in the workshop and it was a course that the students wanted to do. It started with explaining HTML and how it works. This worked fine if students came to every session, but this doesn't happen very often in this environment. We then found that at every session we had to repeat one or two of the sessions that we had previously covered. This was making it difficult to keep the lessons flowing. It was decided that it might be easier to offer the course to a few students at a time and let them work in small groups. This way different groups would be at different levels to complete the necessary coursework and as students come and go there would still be some in the workshop that would be progressing towards completing the coursework. Overall, I have learned a lot from the whole experience: the course and how to implement it, to make it workable. I wonder if there are ways to ensure more continuity for our students, making sure they can attend all sessions, so they can complete their qualification which will enhance their self-esteem and job opportunities for when they leave.

The next two accounts are examples of how you can develop your writing from the Reasoning to the Reconstructing level (equivalent to Critical Reflection or Reflective writing 2 level).

Investigation into dyslexia 1

This investigation refers to a key issue that I have identified to develop my profession-alism as a trainer within the police service. I currently train newly recruited police officers on the Initial Police and Learning Development Programme (IPLDP). I am aware that more students are being recruited to the police service, some of whom have already been diagnosed with dyslexia, or others who are identified during training with this learning difficulty. Although these students are given assistance, by the Students to Achieve Results Team (START), I feel as a classroom trainer I would like to develop my understanding of the learning difficulty, so that I can structure my lessons with *suitable learning activities and resources to support and enhance learning. My research included looking at books and websites. Firstly I explored what dyslexia is. Secondly I investigated means by which to identify some of the signs that a dyslexic student may display, and how to approach these problems. Thirdly in respect of the police service, I made an appointment to see START and discussed with a member of the team, who specifically deals with dyslexia, what procedures are in place and how to assist a student who shows signs of learning difficulties and how to refer them for help. Finally I identified methods of how I can help a student with dyslexia in a classroom environment. This investigation has made me more aware of the learning difficulty and I have identified various aspects of my teaching methods which in future I will change, i.e. asking people to read out loud in the classroom, as this can cause a dyslexic student anxiety. Although I already use a variety of multi-sensory resources in my lessons, I have identified many different resources to aid the dyslexic students and will adapt my lessons in the future, which will enhance their learning and be advantageous to the other students in the classroom.*

Investigation into dyslexia 2

This investigation refers to a key issue that I have identified to develop my profession-alism as a trainer within the police service. I currently train newly recruited police officers on the Initial Police and Learning Development Programme (IPLDP). I am aware of the Disability Discrimination Act (DDA) 1995, which aims to end the discrimination that many disabled people face. This Act has been significantly extended, including by the Disability Discrimination Act 2005. It now gives disabled people rights in the areas of employment and education. As a result, more students are being recruited to the police service who have already been diagnosed with dyslexia. Others, on the other hand, may be identified during training with this learning difficulty. Although these students are given assistance, by the Students to Achieve Results Team (START), I feel as a classroom trainer I would like to develop my understanding of the learning difficulty. At the moment I know very little about dyslexia or of how to meet the needs of dyslexic learners. Although I don't think I'm a bad teacher – feedback is usually positive – when I evaluate my teaching sessions, I sometimes feel I don't differentiate enough to meet the needs of all learners. Therefore, I need to structure my lessons with suitable learning activities and resources to support and enhance learning.

As I enjoy self-study, which I can do at a time convenient to me, my research included looking at books and websites. Firstly I explored what dyslexia is, through this I now have a better understanding of how people are diagnosed with this learning difficulty. This has made a huge impact. As I didn't know too much about the subject, I did consider whether some people use it as an excuse for not working hard enough. I now know that dyslexia is real: something that has been recognised by the organisation but, after discussing it with my colleagues, perhaps not yet by all trainers. Next, I thought it would be really useful if were able to recognise some of the signs or behaviours dyslexic learners might display in class. Of course I'm not an expert but the sooner we can start an intervention programme, the better it is. I discussed this with some of my learners, seeking their opinion. It's all very well for me to think I'm doing the right thing, but how is it for those involved? What is their perspective? They confirmed that their education might have been an easier journey if their dyslexia had been diagnosed at an earlier stage. Thirdly in respect of the police service, I made an appointment to see START and discussed with a member of the team, who specifically deals with dyslexia, what procedures are in place and how to assist a student who shows signs of learning difficulties and how to refer them for help. I also contacted the Dyslexia Association with a view to identify methods of how I can help a student with dyslexia in a classroom environment. This research has made me more aware of the learning difficulty and I have identified various aspects of my teaching methods which in future I will change, i.e. asking people to read out loud in the classroom, as this can cause a dyslexic student anxiety. Although I already use a variety of multi-sensory resources in my lessons, I have identified many different resources to aid the dyslexic students and will adapt my lessons in the future, which will enhance their learning and be advantageous to the other students in the classroom. Given the legislation and current emphasis on meeting individual learners' needs, I feel all trainers within the service should be aware of how to differentiate their teaching, not only to meet the needs of dyslexic learners but also other needs. The support for learners seems to be there at an organisational level but we need to support our learners in class; therefore the trainers need training.

The second account displays an awareness of the social and political context; the view and perspectives of others are taken into account; there is a clear indication of what has been learned from the experience and a critical stance has been adopted. As stated before, the hierarchy is developmental. The majority of new teachers start their reflective writing at the Descriptive level. This is mainly because they don't know how to do it, not because they are not able to do it. Within their time on an Initial Teacher Training programme students develop their writing, with most reaching the Reasoning or Dialogic reflection level (Reflective writing 1) in the second year of the programme. Some, who perhaps are more reflective in nature anyway, reach the Reconstructing or Critical Reflection stage (Reflective writing 2). As you may have noticed, the more reflective accounts tend to be longer, as there is more to consider and write about. Keep this in mind when your word-count is restricted.

To give you more practice in identifying the characteristics of higher-level reflective writing, which you can then apply to your own writing, consider the following examples: at what level do you classify them now and how can they be developed?

TASK TASK **TASK** TASK **TASK** **TASK** TASK **TASK** TASK **TASK** **TASK** TASK

Read the following examples and discuss their level of reflection with a colleague. Do you agree with each other? How can the writing be further developed?

Example 1. A change in role: reflections on a new job

I don't know whether to be happy or sad. Yes I got the job, but in truth am I up to it in all respects? My main concern is that of managing people. I know that I am able to do the job but I ask myself, am I fully prepared to do the job properly? I've researched the topic a little in books and on the internet. I found one article that summed up for me how I feel about my new role, not because it describes how I feel, no, quite the contrary. It describes the behaviours of an effective manager, but it does so in terms that are vague and meaningless. For example, it is suggested that to be an effective manager I should 'respect my own strengths and weaknesses'. This is all very well, but I don't really know what respect means in this context. What will respecting them actually achieve anyway? Another piece of advice is that I should be mindful that 'social-

emotional growth is a never ending process'; that is not particularly useful advice as I can't do anything about it or change it, so what's the point? One behaviour alluded to was to 'clearly communicate rules, goals and expectations'. This I do and always have done, I think, but the question is, what rules, how many rules and how should I see they are adhered to? I am not a disciplinarian; provided everyone is happy and if they are then they are working well, if they work well I am happy; as for rules, they are not important for me. In relation to goals I wonder whose goals I should be communicating. I mustn't be too harsh as there is a line that suggests I should 'respond to behaviours consistently and predictably'. I can go along with the 'consistently' but why 'predictably', it sounds like the behaviour of an automaton. Then I am faced with the advice that I should 'Discriminate between issues of responsibility and problem ownership.' You what?! And then it hits me, just look at what I am doing, writing about stuff that has no actual value and I am getting wound up by it and I wonder, just for a moment about where I am at right now.

Now I realise the mistake I am making, it's the fact that I have surfed the net, found a pile of meaningless information and have stupidly taken it to mean something of value. And I feel that it is getting to me just a bit. I suppose it is the combination of the new job, trying to prepare myself and feeling hugely under pressure. It's not the fear of the unknown, because I know what the job entails mostly. The issue here is, I suppose, how do I fit into the job exactly? There is advice to be found, but I feel it is not helping me.

I have made a list of the things that bother me the most. Surprisingly the thing that came out on top is giving appraisals. It wasn't until I gave some thought to what my issues were that it came up. I should have thought it through because it's like a recurring dream I have recently where I am doing an appraisal and I just can't think of anything to say, nothing, and just look at the papers in my hands. Then the member of staff in the dream starts to laugh, saying, 'You don't know how to do it do you, you've not got the first idea have you?' Then they leave the office laughing and telling others outside that I couldn't do it. It's the managing people side of things that I now realise is the trouble for me. Managing courses, schemes of work, students, etc., is no problem at all. Where I feel I need help is managing staff.

As a result I have decided to request training. I will discuss this with my line manager and see which courses are available to me. I don't know why I didn't do this before.

Example 2. Action research: pictorial representation

I teach National Diploma/Certificate courses in art and design. As part of the Historical and Contextual Studies Unit, I felt it was important to develop resources on pictorial representations of gender, (dis)ability and ethnicity, as I found that some of my students' experiences are very limited. Latest government legislation and emphasis on diversity requires a closer look at how these categories are represented in art.

The value and effectiveness of the resources were assessed through pilot lessons with two different groups of level 3 learners. The response of the first group allowed me to refine both the visual material and the learning activities, which were subsequently presented to the second group. There were several changes that were introduced after the earlier class.

The number of images was reduced because there was insufficient time to discuss them all.

The Marc Quinn sculpture of 'Alison Lapper Pregnant' on the vacant plinth in Trafalgar Square was omitted because it was too well known and the students had formed prior opinions of the work.

There was less emphasis on organised group work because all students were prepared to engage with the topic and preferred to make individual contributions.

Students in both groups actively participated in the class and were able to draw their own, often highly intelligent inferences from the images and the questions that accompanied them. My own role, that of the lecturer, became one of summarising their observations on a flipchart, providing supplementary information about the slides when asked to do so and occasionally asking questions to draw out the implications of what learner had said. Students were quick to make a connection between Hugh S's experiences as part of a charity fundraising campaign and the image entitled 'Piss on Pity' by Semena Rana. There was general agreement within both groups that Witkin and Arbus disseminated negative images of disabled people because they either placed them in a bizarre context that denied their humanity (Witkin) or by deliberately selecting images that treated their behaviour as abnormal (Arbus). One student remarked: 'that's awful – they've chosen to make photos of them not doing normal things'. Lambert and Rama, on the other hand, were perceived as depicting their subjects as 'just like us', either in working situations, interacting with others or individually, in dignified portraits such as Lambert's 'Mary', which one group described as 'serious and thoughtful'. Of all the images in the sequence, those of Joel Peter Witkins attracted the strongest criticism. Faced with Witkin's 'Il Santo Oscuro' (the unknown saint), several of the students remarked, 'is that a person?' or 'is that a human being?' One learner's indignant claim that 'he treats his models like freaks' corresponds exactly to David Heveys' celebrated argument that artists like Witkin and Arbus 'enfreak' the disabled. Freaks, argued Hevey, are objects of fear, curiosity or revulsion and, as such, are socially excluded (Hevey, 1992 and 1997 passim).

Learners were initially uncertain when faced with Marc Quinn's series of white marble figures of disabled adults. When Quinn's pieces were juxtaposed with traditional sculptures, however, students from both groups suggested that Quinn was trying to present an alternative to the way artists have usually represented the human body. They implied that the traditional works provided an ideal body image and in the case of Polykleitos's 'Doryphorus', that was absolutely the case, since the sculpture was created in order to exemplify what Polykleitos believed to be the perfect set of proportions for the male body. Both groups recognised that Quinn was setting out to challenge that ideal by using the same material – flawless white marble – to represent bodily difference. The juxtaposition of Quinn's 'The Kiss' with the same subject by Auguste Rodin provoked animated discussion. The conclusion was that while Rodin represented a normal view of sexuality, Quinn's sculpture dealt with disabled sexuality – something that the students had rarely, if ever, seen represented in the mainstream media.

In the closing stages of the class, learners were asked the questions 'Why is it important to study the ways in which disabled people are represented?' Their replies showed that they were aware by the end of the class that images of disability play a significant part in shaping attitudes to the disabled. Some referred back to High S's text and to his reasons for studying film and media representations of the subject. When they were asked to speculate about the reasons why some of the artists decided to challenge negative images of disability, most responses were framed in terms of social justice but one or two students in both groups asked whether those artists were themselves disabled. One suggested that the disabled have to be able to speak for themselves. This remark echoed David Hevey's contribution to a discussion of Witkin's work on the BBC2 programme, Late Review. He insisted that images such as 'Il Santo Oscuro' would eventually become unacceptable, but only when disabled people themselves have a voice in the discourse (BBC2, 1996).

In both sessions learners were able to compare the images related to disability with those studied in previous classes on equality issues: one student, for example, made the point that a white photographer could no longer degrade a black person in the way that the able-bodied Witkin had treated his disabled models. From next year the topic and material will become incorporated into the historical/contextual curriculum. I also propose to enlist the students' help in developing the slide resources at our disposal by asking them to collect pictures from art, advertising or the media that they feel might be relevant to the subject.

Example 3. Improving my teaching

I teach adults with learning difficulties and disabilities (ALDD) in the community adult education department of a further education college. I am interested in developing my own teaching by promoting literacy and comprehension of written text using signs, symbols and games. I am aware that When considering resources to promote effective learning the question of students' abilities to use the resources must be surely a central issue *(Armitage et al., 2006, page 149), hence my interest. If the students are not looking at our carefully prepared handouts and worksheets, I have to consider why; what are the reasons. I asked my fellow tutors whether they have found using symbols has improved the clarity and comprehension of their handouts. The overall consensus was that using symbols requires us to think more carefully about what we are writing, simplifying the content, but it does not necessarily improve the student's comprehension. I didn't expect this.*

I assumed that our students would be more interested in a handout which is visually attractive, as 75% of what we learn comes through what we see (Reece and Walker, 2006, page 156). I assumed that the students will pay more attention to the pictures even if they do understand the written words underneath. The lower-ability students in parti-cular, will choose the 'Widgit' sheet in preference to one which has no pictures. However, we have not taught our students to read the pictures or symbols. It could be that while some symbols may be easily recognisable, it is not realistic to put a page of symbols in front of a reader and expect him or her to understand it quickly. Pictures don't necessarily mean comprehension. What I have learned from this is that I have to explain the symbols and pictures first, and check the learners' understanding. This is something that has come up in my assessed lessons as well. I am new to teaching and don't always know where to pitch things. I mainly teach cookery. Here, there is the advantage that real objects are the ingredients for that recipe. I also use the ingredients to promote discussion and to see that the learners recognise each ingredient and understand how it will be prepared. We now 'read' the recipe, using the worksheet with symbols and pictures, at the beginning of the lesson. Those students with limited literacy are asked to identify the pictures, while those who are able to read are asked to read those ingredients and instructions which have no picture/symbol attached. Thus all students participate in the lesson and the task is differentiated according to ability. Once the written recipe has been discussed we move onto real ingredients, we continue to refer back to the recipe for the preparation of the ingredients and cooking methods.

The best results were obtained for those nouns which are commonly used and for which the symbols are a direct representation, i.e. knife, fork or spoon. For one of my sessions the learning objective was for the students to be able to read a set of symbols, which would allow them understand one of the recipes. I chose the Fruity Muffins recipe, as I know from experience that the students all enjoy making cakes, and then chose those symbols I thought they could identify. I next gave them the same words to read with no visual clues or prompts. One student became distressed during this process, despite a lot of reassurance, and although there were only eight words to read, the task was beyond her. In future, I will be more selective in who I give the words to read. I felt awful about the student's distress, how would I feel if I was asked to do something that I wasn't feeling competent in. I need to be more sensitive, as I don't want this to happen again.

In conclusion, carrying out this study has been very beneficial to my professional development. I have extended my knowledge of ICT and how to use a particular program more effectively, which makes this resource far more beneficial to my learners. As although I was aware of 'Widgit' and did use it to produce resources for my lessons I now know how to better incorporate its use, through worksheets and games, to promote and help develop the literacy of the ALDD with whom I work. I have developed strategies to differentiate so that all students can participate at their own ability.

My action plan is to continue to develop games, which I will use to reinforce learning and help promote literacy. I will also teach my students to look at the pictures, not assuming that they will understand just because they are pictures. One student in particular has made great progress in understanding the recipes in cookery as she now reads the pictures. I believe that with regular and consistent teaching, the majority of adults with literacy difficulties would benefit from this system. The less able will probably continue to need support of the symbols, but more able students may be able to improve their independent reading ability. I have learned a lot and I would like to further develop my skills. There are more resources I would like to try and there is a course I would like to enrol on. However, there is a money implication. I am aware that funding for the type of classes I teach is not secure. That is not just for my classes but for the whole of Community Ed. We don't quite know where we stand and what our future entails: do we still have a job next year? I know this is not so much a college policy as a national issue. I feel we owe it, as a society, to support those of us with learning difficulties and disabilities, to be able to fulfil their potential. I feel there is a tension between policies to secure inclusion for our learners and funding issues.

Example 1: Very descriptive with some personal reflection.
Example 2: Although of a much higher academic level of writing, it is still largely descriptive with some reference to socio-political issues.
Example 3: Still some description, but used to set the context. Higher level of reflection, identifying what has been learned and how to further develop skills. Awareness shown of political situation which may have impact.

A SUMMARY OF **KEY POINTS**

In this chapter we have looked at the following key points:

> **Explained different levels of reflective writing as described by the three frameworks referred to:**

1. **Hatton and Smith (1995): Descriptive writing; Descriptive reflection; Dialogic reflection; and Critical reflection.**

2. **Based on Moon (2004): Descriptive writing; Descriptive account with some reflection; Reflective writing 1 and 2.**

3. **Samuels (2008), based on Bain et al.: five-point scale – Reporting; Responding; Relating; Reasoning, and Reconstructing.**

> **Identified the characteristics of each level of reflective writing.**

> **Described how to develop a reflective account to the next level, giving you the opportunity to practise this by working with the examples.**

> **Encouraged you to critically evaluate your own writing, identifying how to improve it.**

REFERENCES AND FURTHER READING REFERENCES AND FURTHER READING

Hatton, N and Smith, D (1995) *Reflection in teacher education: towards definition and implementation.* University of Sydney: School of Teaching and Curriculum Studies.

Moon, J (2004) *A handbook of reflective and experiential learning theory and practice.* London: RoutledgeFalmer.

Samuels, M (2008) *Frameworks/tools for assessing levels of reflection* www.thewestminsterpartnershipcett.org.uk/. Accessed 12 August 2008.

To conclude

This book has been a journey. It started with giving you an overview of the general theory and an explanation for why you even have to consider professional reflective practice. It has explained the benefits of being reflective, especially with the links to learning and with regard to maintaining your professional standing. It has described the process of professional reflective practice and has given you some useful strategies, mnemonics and techniques to get you started. However, all reflection requires a level of self-awareness. This may not always be a comfortable process: looking at your own values, behaviours, questioning them and acknowledging where they came from, may be a bit unsettling. It requires honesty and commitment. However, it is not about judging you, merely an exercise in getting to know yourself better. Only then can you take control and identify what you need to work on, either in the knowledge, skills or attitude department, and move on.

For the purpose of this book, your reflections are strongly linked to your CPD; that is what you have to write about to meet the regulations. Therefore, the next part of the book gave you some examples of a range of activities that other people have used to count towards their 30 hours (or pro-rata equivalent) of CPD. Next is how to record it. The book offers some pro formas to give you structure, something to start with. The Institute for Learning have developed Reflect, where you can record your entries online. Research shows that more and more people use the computer; the Appendix offers a useful IT jargon buster which explains the jargon. Finally, we looked at how you can improve the quality of your reflective writing. Most trainee teachers start by being descriptive, just telling what happened. Later on, they 'stand back' from the situation and incorporate different perspectives, make links to theory, they become more critical and aware of socio-political issues, which influence their practice.

As stated, there is no end to being reflective.

Appendix

IT jargon buster

Address	The location of a source of information, where to find something, e.g. www.qtls.net
ADSL	Asynchronous Digital Subscriber Line – Broadband
Aggregate	To collect things under various tags
Asset	A record of a completed activity within Reflect, stored within the account of the owner
Attachment	A document that is bolted onto an email message
Bandwidth	The amount of information available to you – the bigger the band, the more information you get
Banner	An advert
Broadband	Fast internet
Browser	The long list you see when you do a search on something
Click	Pressing your left mouse button once
Connection	Gaining access to the internet
Cookies	Files that record where you have been on the internet
Cursor	The bit like an arrow that you can move around the screen with your mouse
Database	A file that is used to store information
Desktop	Your screen when you first start the computer with the small icons on
Domain	Small groups within the internet e.g. ac.uk, gov.uk
Domain name	An address for a place on the internet
Double-click	Pressing your left mouse button twice quickly
Download	To copy file and documents from the web to your computer
Driver	Something that controls something else like a printer
Email	A message sent from one computer to another
Emoticon	A facial expression like a smiley face e.g. :) ☺
FAQ	Short for Frequently Asked Questions, where you can find the answers to specific questions
File	A document or program
Firewall	A program to keep hackers out of your computer
GIF	Graphics Interchange Format – a picture on the web
Gigabyte	A thousand megabytes
Hacker	Someone who breaks into another computer or network
Hard disk	This stores your files; also called the hard drive
Hit	A term for when someone looks at a web page
Home page	The first page you get when you visit a website
HTML	Hyper Text Markup – a language used in a web page
HTTP	Hyper Text Transfer Protocol – a set of rules
Hyperlink	Something highlighted like blue underlined words or a picture which links to another page on the net
Icon	A symbol on your desktop

Internet	*A collection of all the interconnected networks in the world*
Internet Explorer	*Used for searching on the net*
IP address	*Internet Protocol Address – your computer's unique number*
ISP	*Internet Service Provider – the company which give you a connection to the internet*
JPEG	*Joint Photographic Experts Group – used for photos*
Kb	*A kilobyte – 1024 bytes*
Link	*The door to another place on the web (hyperlink)*
Login	*Putting in your username and password to access a protected website*
Mailing list	*You can elect to be placed on a mailing list to receive messages to your email address*
Megabyte (MB)	*A unit of data comprising of 1024 kb*
MP3	*Music or audio information is stored on an MP3 file*
MPEG	*Motion Picture Experts Group – used for video files*
Multimedia	*A combination of different media within a single document*
Netiquette	*Internet etiquette*
Network	*Connected computers which exchange information*
POP	*Post Office Protocol – a method of storing and returning email*
Portal	*A website designed to lead you to other websites*
Provider	*An Internet Service Provider, or ISP*
Right-click	*To press the button on the right-hand side of the mouse.*
Search engine	*A tool for searching information on the internet e.g. ask.com, google.com*
Server	*A computer which provides files and other services to other computers*
Site	*A collection of web pages*
SMTP	*Simple Mail Transfer Protocol – enables messages to be delivered*
Spam	*Unwanted messages from people you don't know*
Surfing	*Exploring the web*
Tag	*Tags are the things that allow you to group together your assets in Reflect*
Taskbar	*The bar in the Windows operating system that is shown at the bottom of the screen*
Text box	*A box in which you can type*
Trojan	*A sneaky computer program that is designed to disrupt your computer (as in 'Trojan horse')*
Upload	*The opposite of download – to transfer information (files) from a PC to a network or the internet*
URL	*Uniform Resource Locator – an address of an internet site, e.g. http:// www.qtls.net*
Virus	*A harmful program that gets into your computer via the internet*
Webfolio	*An evidence-based web-publishing system where you can publish things to other people across the internet*
Webmail	*Email controlled from a website, so you can access it wherever you are*
Webpage	*A document on the web*
Windows	*An operating system which enables you to communicate with your computer*
Worm	*A virus*
ZIP	*A file that has been squeezed up to make it smaller and easier to send*